1961

The Day You Were Born
U.K. Yearbook

ISBN: 9798567573457

© Diamond Publishing 2020
All Rights Reserved

INDEX

	Page
Calendar	4
People in High Office	5
British News & Events	9
Worldwide News & Events	17
Births - U.K. Personalities	26
Notable British Deaths	33
Popular Music	35
Top 5 Films	41
Sporting Winners	52
Cost of Living	59
Cartoons	68

FIRST EDITION

1961

January
M	T	W	T	F	S	S
						1
2	3	4	5	6	7	8
9	10	11	12	13	14	15
16	17	18	19	20	21	22
23	24	25	26	27	28	29
30	31					

◔:1 ◐:10 ●:16 ◑:23 ◯:31

February
M	T	W	T	F	S	S
		1	2	3	4	5
6	7	8	9	10	11	12
13	14	15	16	17	18	19
20	21	22	23	24	25	26
27	28					

◐:8 ●:15 ◑:22

March
M	T	W	T	F	S	S
		1	2	3	4	5
6	7	8	9	10	11	12
13	14	15	16	17	18	19
20	21	22	23	24	25	26
27	28	29	30	31		

◯:2 ◐:10 ●:16 ◑:24

April
M	T	W	T	F	S	S
					1	2
3	4	5	6	7	8	9
10	11	12	13	14	15	16
17	18	19	20	21	22	23
24	25	26	27	28	29	30

◯:1 ◐:8 ●:15 ◑:22 ◯:30

May
M	T	W	T	F	S	S
1	2	3	4	5	6	7
8	9	10	11	12	13	14
15	16	17	18	19	20	21
22	23	24	25	26	27	28
29	30	31				

◐:7 ●:14 ◑:22 ◯:30

June
M	T	W	T	F	S	S
			1	2	3	4
5	6	7	8	9	10	11
12	13	14	15	16	17	18
19	20	21	22	23	24	25
26	27	28	29	30		

◐:5 ●:13 ◑:21 ◯:28

July
M	T	W	T	F	S	S
					1	2
3	4	5	6	7	8	9
10	11	12	13	14	15	16
17	18	19	20	21	22	23
24	25	26	27	28	29	30
31						

◐:5 ●:12 ◑:21 ◯:27

August
M	T	W	T	F	S	S
	1	2	3	4	5	6
7	8	9	10	11	12	13
14	15	16	17	18	19	20
21	22	23	24	25	26	27
28	29	30	31			

◐:3 ●:11 ◑:19 ◯:26

September
M	T	W	T	F	S	S
				1	2	3
4	5	6	7	8	9	10
11	12	13	14	15	16	17
18	19	20	21	22	23	24
25	26	27	28	29	30	

◐:2 ●:10 ◑:17 ◯:24

October
M	T	W	T	F	S	S
						1
2	3	4	5	6	7	8
9	10	11	12	13	14	15
16	17	18	19	20	21	22
23	24	25	26	27	28	29
30	31					

◐:1 ●:9 ◑:17 ◯:23 ◐:31

November
M	T	W	T	F	S	S
		1	2	3	4	5
6	7	8	9	10	11	12
13	14	15	16	17	18	19
20	21	22	23	24	25	26
27	28	29	30			

●:8 ◑:15 ◯:22 ◐:30

December
M	T	W	T	F	S	S
				1	2	3
4	5	6	7	8	9	10
11	12	13	14	15	16	17
18	19	20	21	22	23	24
25	26	27	28	29	30	31

●:7 ◑:14 ◯:22 ◐:30

People in High Office

Monarch - Queen Elizabeth II
Reign: 6th February 1952 - Present
Predecessor: King George VI
Heir Apparent: Charles, Prince of Wales

United Kingdom

Prime Minister
Harold Macmillan
Conservative Party
10th January 1957 - 19th October 1963

Australia	Canada	United States
Prime Minister **Sir Robert Menzies** 19th December 1949 - 26th January 1966	Prime Minister **John Diefenbaker** 21st June 1957 - 22nd April 1963	President **John F. Kennedy** 20th January 1961 - 22nd November 1963

	Brazil	President Juscelino Kubitschek (1956-1961) Jânio Quadros (1961) Ranieri Mazzilli (1961) João Goulart (1961-1964)
	China	Chairman Liu Shaoqi (1959-1968)
	France	President Charles de Gaulle (1959-1969)
	India	Prime Minister Jawaharlal Nehru (1947-1964)
	Ireland	Taoiseach Seán Lemass (1959-1966)
	Israel	Prime Minister David Ben-Gurion (1955-1963)
	Italy	Prime Minister Amintore Fanfani (1960-1963)
	Japan	Prime Minister Hayato Ikeda (1960-1964)

	Mexico	President Adolfo López Mateos (1958-1964)
	New Zealand	Prime Minister Keith Holyoake (1960-1972)
	Pakistan	President Ayub Khan (1958-1969)
	South Africa	Prime Minister Hendrik Verwoerd (1958-1966)
	Soviet Union	Communist Party Leader Nikita Khrushchev (1953-1964)
	Spain	President Francisco Franco (1938-1973)
	Turkey	Prime Minister Cemal Gürsel (1960-1961) Fahrettin Özdilek (1961) İsmet İnönü (1961-1962)
	West Germany	Chancellor Konrad Adenauer (1949-1963)

BRITISH NEWS & EVENTS

JAN

1st	Britain's tiniest coin the farthing, in use since the thirteenth century, ceases to be legal tender.
1st	The political pressure group The Monday Club is established by four young Conservative Party members. Paul Bristol, a 24-year-old shipbroker, becomes the club's first chairman.
1st	The Betting and Gaming Act 1960 (passed on the 1st September 1960) comes into force permitting the operation of commercial bingo halls and gambling for small sums in games of skill.
7th	Five members of the Soviet Portland Spy Ring are arrested in London; they are charged with espionage two days later at Bow Street Magistrates Court.

7th January: The pilot episode of The Avengers, "Hot Snow", debuts on ITV. *Fun facts: The Avengers ran until the 21st May 1969 (161 episodes) and was shown in more than 90 countries. Pictured: Patrick Macnee (series 1-6) and Honor Blackman (series 2-3).*

FEB

5th	The Sunday Telegraph newspaper is published for the first time.

FEB

9th February: The Beatles perform at the legendary Cavern Club in Liverpool for the first time and are paid £5 for the unadvertised lunchtime appearance. *Fun facts: The Beatles made 292 appearances at the Cavern Club during 1961, 1962 and 1963. Their final appearance there was on the 3rd August 1963 and took place just one month after the group recorded "She Loves You", and six months before their first trip to the United States. Photo: The Beatles onstage at the Cavern Club in February 1961. (L-R) George Harrison, Paul McCartney, Pete Best and John Lennon.*

19th	Outside the Belgian embassy in London mounted police break up a demonstration protesting the murder of the ex-Congolese Prime Minister Patrice Lumumba.

MAR

6th	In London Carline Cabs introduce the first minicabs to the capital. Carline, exploiting a loophole in the 1869 Carriage Act, operate by responding to phone calls made to the main office which are then relayed to the driver. *Interesting facts: In the first week Carline Cabs' fleet of 12 Ford Anglia 105Es carried 500 passengers. The minicab drivers charged a rate two thirds of that of a black cab and promised a greater service to London's outer suburbs.*
8th	Edwin Bush is arrested in London for the capital stabbing of 59-year-old Elsie May Batten on the 3rd March 1961. *Follow up: Bush, the first British criminal to be identified by the Identikit facial composite system, was convicted and then executed at Pentonville Prison in London on the 6th July 1961, aged 21. He was the last person to be hanged at Pentonville Prison.*
9th	The Minister of Health Enoch Powell, in his famous "Water Towers" speech to a Conservative Party conference, proposes closing down large traditional psychiatric hospitals in favour of more community-based care.

MAR

13th	The five members of the Portland Spy Ring, Harry Houghton, Ethel Gee, Gordon Lonsdale, and Americans Morris and Lona Cohen, go on trial at the Old Bailey accused of passing nuclear secrets to the Soviet Union. Houghton and Gee are sentenced to 15 years in prison, the Cohens to 20 years, and Lonsdale (the mastermind) to 25 years.
13th	Cyprus, which gained its independence from the United Kingdom on the 16th August 1960, joins the Commonwealth of Nations.
13th	Black and white £5 notes (printed on one side only) cease to be legal tender.
15th	South Africa announces it will withdraw from the Commonwealth of Nations upon becoming a republic on the 31st May 1961. The country's move follows a storm of criticism for its racial policies by Commonwealth members. *Notes: On the 25th October 1993, South Africa was invited to re-join the Commonwealth of Nations after prolonged talks on constitutional reform between the government, the African National Congress (ANC) and other key liberation movements. It re-joined on the 1st June 1994.*

17th March: Jaguar founder Sir William Lyons debuts the first E-Type model at the Geneva International Motor Show to huge excitement from the world's press. *Fun facts: With a launch price of around £2,250 (2020: £52,305) the E-Types beautiful bodywork set it apart from anything else on the road with Enzo Ferrari famously describing it as "the most beautiful car in the world". During the 14 years the E-Type was in production over 70,000 cars were sold. Pictured: Sir William Lyons at the 1961 launch of the E-Type to the press in Geneva.*

25th	Nicolaus Silver wins the 115th Grand National 5 lengths ahead of defending champion Merryman II. Ridden by Bobby Beasley, Nicolaus Silver is the first grey to win the race for 90 years.

APR

8th	The British passenger ship Dara blows up and sinks off Dubai; of the 819 passengers and crew on board 238 are killed. *Follow up: A British Admiralty court concluded more than a year after the disaster that an anti-tank mine, "deliberately placed by a person or persons unknown", had "almost certainly" caused the explosion.*
17th	Tottenham Hotspur win the Football League First Division Championship for the second time with a 2-1 win over Sheffield Wednesday.
27th	Sierra Leone gains its independence from Britain.

MAY

1st	Betting shops become legal under terms of the Betting and Gaming Act 1960.
1st	A fire at the Top Storey Club in Bolton results in nineteen deaths. Changes are quickly made to the Licensing Act 1961 in an attempt to improve fire safety.
6th	Tottenham Hotspur becomes the first English football team of the century, and only the third in history, to win the double of the league title and FA Cup with their 2-0 victory over Leicester City in the FA Cup Final. *Fun facts: The two previous teams who achieved the league and FA Cup double were Preston North End in 1889 and Aston Villa in 1897.*
8th	George Blake is sentenced to 42 years imprisonment for spying having been found guilty of being a double agent for the Soviet Union. *NB: At the time 42 years was the longest sentence (excluding life terms) ever handed down by a British court. Follow up: Five years into Blake's imprisonment in Wormwood Scrubs he escaped and fled to the Soviet Union. As of 2020, aged 97, he was living in Moscow on a KGB pension.*
17th	Guildford Cathedral, designed by Edward Maufe and built between 1936 and 1966, is consecrated in the presence of The Queen, The Duke of Edinburgh, the Archbishop of Canterbury and a packed congregation from all parts of the Diocese.
28th	Peter Benenson's "The Forgotten Prisoners" is published in The Observer and is reprinted in newspapers across the world. This article will later be seen as the beginning of the founding of the human rights organisation Amnesty International.
31st	Arthur Michael Ramsey is appointed the 100th Archbishop of Canterbury, a position he holds until 1974.
31st	South Africa becomes a republic and officially leaves the Commonwealth of Nations.

JUN

8th	Prince Edward, Duke of Kent, the eldest son of Prince George, Duke of Kent, and Princess Marina of Greece and Denmark, marries Katharine Worsley at York Minster.
14th	The Ministry of Transport unveils the new "panda" crossings to be introduced in 1962. They will have push button controls for pedestrians and are to be installed due to the rising number of accidents on uncontrolled zebra crossings. *Fun facts: The first panda crossing opened on York Road (near Waterloo Station), London on the 2nd April 1962. The panda crossing would eventually be replaced by the X-way (1967) and the pelican crossing (1969).*

JUN

19th	The British protectorate ends in Kuwait and it becomes an emirate.
22nd	The Beatles, with English singer Tony Sheridan on lead vocals, record My Bonnie and The Saints at the Friedrich-Ebert-Halle in Hamburg. *Fun facts: My Bonnie was released as a single (with The Saints on the B-side) in Germany in October 1961. Credited to Tony Sheridan and The Beat Brothers, it reached No.32 on the national chart. The German import became popular in Liverpool and came to the attention of Brian Epstein who subsequently went to see the Beatles at the Cavern Club. Although he had no experience of artist management he signed them to a five-year contract on the 24th January 1962. Epstein insisted The Beatles abandon their scruff-image in favour of a new clean-cut style with identical suits and haircuts, and persuaded George Martin of EMI to produce their records. Within months the Beatles were international stars.*
27th	Kuwait requests help from the U.K. after Iraqi president Abd al-Karim Qasim announces he is going to annex Kuwait. A British military operation to support the newly independent state of Kuwait, Operation Vantage, takes place three days later. *Follow up: Iraq did not attack and the British forces were replaced by the Arab League. Iraq recognised Kuwaiti independence in 1963.*

JUL

4th	Barclays open Britain's first computer centre for banking at Drummond Street, London.
8th	Angela Mortimer beats Christine Truman in an all-British women's Wimbledon final.

21st July: The Runcorn Widnes Bridge over the River Mersey (now known as the Silver Jubilee Bridge) is opened by Princess Alexandra. *Fun facts: Costing £2,433,000 the bridge was built using 5,900 tons of steel, 7,500 tons of concrete and 720,000 rivets. At the time of its construction it had the third longest steel arch span in the world at 330m. Photo: The Runcorn Widnes Bridge nearing completion (8th June 1961).*

JUL

25th — The Government calls for a voluntary "pay pause" in wage increases in an attempt to improve Britain's competitive position in world markets. *NB: The pay pause was brought to an end on the 31st March 1962.*

AUG

3rd — The Suicide Act 1961 receives Royal assent and decriminalises the act of suicide in England and Wales (so that those who fail in the attempt to kill themselves can no longer be prosecuted).

6th August: Race driver Stirling Moss scores his 16th and final Formula 1 victory in the German Grand Prix at the Nürburgring. *Fun facts: An inductee into the International Motorsports Hall of Fame, Moss won 212 of the 529 races he entered across several categories of competition and has been described as "the greatest driver never to win the World Championship". In a seven-year span between 1955 and 1961 he finished as the Formula 1 championship runner-up four times and was placed third the other three times. Photo: Moss in his race winning Lotus 18/21 at the Nürburgring.*

17th — The Handley Page HP.115, a delta wing aircraft built by Handley Page (part of the British supersonic aircraft research programme sponsored by the Ministry of Supply), makes its first flight at the Royal Aircraft Establishment Bedford. *Fun fact: Neil Armstrong was due to fly the HP.115 as a test pilot in 1962 but after his selection as an astronaut NASA refused him permission. He did eventually get to fly it though on the 22nd June 1970.*

19th — Two days of race riots occur in Middlesbrough. Trouble had flared after 25-year-old Asian crane driver Hussain Said had been arrested accused of the murder of 18-year-old Jeffrey Hunt. *Follow up: Said was eventually found not guilty on the direction of the judge who declared there was insufficient evidence to support a guilty verdict.*

AUG

- **23rd** — Police launch a manhunt for the perpetrator of the A6 murder who shot dead 36-year-old scientist Michael Gregsten and paralysed his mistress Valerie Storie. *Follow up: James Hanratty was found guilty and hanged by executioner Harry Allen at Bedford on the 4th April 1962.*
- **25th** — Police in Birmingham launch a murder inquiry after the body of missing 15-year-old biscuit factory worker Jacqueline Thomas is found on an allotment in the Alum Rock area of the city. *Follow up: The crime remained unsolved for over four decades until a cold case review in the 2000s. In 2007, 70-year-old Anthony Hall - already serving a life sentence for the murder of another teenager - was charged with Thomas's murder. However, a judge subsequently ruled the charge should be stayed owing to the length of time that had passed since the incident. Hall subsequently died in prison.*
- **31st** — The film Victim, directed by Basil Dearden and notable as the first English-language film to use the word "homosexual", premieres in London.

SEP

- **16th** — During a Glasgow Rangers football match at Ibrox Park a crush of fans on stairway 13 kills two people and injures scores of others.
- **17th** — At a CND rally in Trafalgar Square police arrest 1,314 anti-nuclear protesters during a sit-down by 12,000. A simultaneous protest at Holy Loch results in 300 arrests.
- **19th** — The first Mothercare shop opens on Thames Street in Kingston upon Thames, Surrey (now Greater London); it was conceived after Iraqi-born businessman Selim Zilkha noticed a gap in the market for shops specialising in goods for parents.
- **21st** — Forty-two-year-old Argentinian swimmer Antonio Albertondo completes the first double crossing of English Channel in a time of 43 hours 5 minutes.

OCT

- Acker Bilk's "Stranger on the Shore" is released and becomes the UK's biggest-selling instrumental single of all time selling 1.13 million copies.
- **1st** — The religious programme Songs of Praise is broadcast for the first time on BBC Television. Today it is one of the longest running series of its genre on television anywhere in the world.
- **9th** — Skelmersdale, a small Lancashire town fifteen miles north-east of Liverpool, is designated as a new town. It is the first in the second wave of designations and will rehouse families from inner city slums on Merseyside.
- **10th** — A volcanic eruption on the South Atlantic British overseas territory of Tristan da Cunha causes the island's entire population of 264 individuals to be evacuated to Britain. *Follow up: The islanders arrived in the U.K. to a big press reception and were settled in an old Royal Air Force camp near Calshot, Hampshire. The following year a Royal Society expedition reported that the islands capital, Edinburgh of the Seven Seas, had survived the eruption and most families returned in 1963. Fun fact: Tristan da Cunha is the most remote inhabited archipelago in the world, lying approximately 1,511 miles (2,432 km) off the coast of Cape Town in South Africa, 1,343 miles (2,161 km) from Saint Helena and 2,166 miles (3,486 km) off the coast of the Falkland Islands.*

OCT

25th — The first edition of Private Eye, the satirical and current affairs news magazine, is published in London.

31st — Hurricane Hattie devastates British Honduras causing widespread damage and the deaths of 307 people. *Note: Due to the destruction and loss of life attributed to the hurricane the name Hattie was retired by the World Meteorological Organisation and will never again be used for an Atlantic hurricane.*

NOV

8th — In a referendum on Sunday opening of public houses in Wales, the counties of Anglesey, Caernarfonshire, Cardiganshire, Carmarthenshire, Denbighshire, Merionethshire, Montgomeryshire and Pembrokeshire all vote to stay "dry" and to oppose the Sunday sale of alcohol.

9th November: At the Lyceum Theatre in London Miss United Kingdom, Welsh-born Rosemarie Frankland, becomes the first British winner of the Miss World beauty pageant. She is crowned by Bob Hope who remarks that she is the most beautiful girl he has ever seen. *Fun facts: Frankland also finished as first runner-up at the Miss Universe pageant four months earlier at the Miami Beach Auditorium in Florida - had she won it she would not have been eligible to enter the Miss World pageant.*

27th — The RAF participates in air drops of food to flood victims in Somalia.

DEC

4th — Health Minister Enoch Powell announces that the oral contraceptive Conovid will be available to women on the NHS at a subsidised price of two shillings per month.

9th — Tanganyika gains its independence from the United Kingdom.

13th — The film musical The Young Ones, starring Cliff Richard, Robert Morley and Carole Gray, premieres at the Warner Theatre in London's West End.

21st — American President John F. Kennedy and British Prime Minister Harold Macmillan meet in Bermuda.

75 WORLDWIDE NEWS & EVENTS

1. 3rd January: A Douglas DC-3C (Aero Flight 311) crashes near Kvevlax in Finland killing all 25 people on board. *Follow up: An investigation reveals that both pilots are intoxicated and should not have been flying. The disaster remains the deadliest civilian aviation accident in Finnish history.*
2. 4th January: Danish barbers' assistants in Copenhagen end their 33-year strike (the longest recorded strike in history).
3. 8th January: A referendum in France convincingly approves Charles de Gaulle's policies on independence for Algeria.
4. 15th January: Berry Gordy signs The Supremes to Motown Records. *Fun facts: The Supremes, founded as a quartet called The Primettes in 1959, were the most commercially successful of Motown's acts and are to date America's most successful vocal group with 12 No.1 singles on the Billboard Hot 100.*

5. 20th January: Democrat John F. Kennedy is sworn in as the 35th President of the United States at the East Portico of the United States Capitol in Washington, D.C. During his famous inauguration address, Kennedy, the youngest candidate ever elected to the presidency (aged 43) and the country's first Catholic president, declared that "the torch has been passed to a new generation of Americans" and appealed to Americans to "ask not what your country can do for you, ask what you can do for your country."

6. 31st January: Ham, a 5-year-old male chimpanzee, is rocketed into space from Cape Canaveral in Florida. Part of the U.S. space program's Project Mercury, Ham is the first hominid to be launched into space. After a flight lasting 16 minutes and 39 seconds, Ham's capsule splashes down in the Atlantic Ocean and is recovered by a rescue ship later that day. The capsule does suffer a partial loss of pressure during the flight but Ham's space suit prevents him from suffering any harm - his only physical injury is a bruised nose. *Fun facts: Officially, Astrochimp Ham was known as No.65 before his flight and only renamed Ham upon his successful return to Earth. Among his handlers though, No.65 had been known as "Chop Chop Chang". Photo: Ham is greeted by the commander of the recovery ship, USS Donner.*

7. 1st February: The first test launch of the Minuteman-I intercontinental ballistic missile takes place from Cape Canaveral Air Force Station in Florida.
8. 12th February: The USSR launches Venera 1 towards Venus. *Follow up: The spacecraft becomes the first to fly past Venus on the 19th May, however, radio contact with the probe is lost before the flyby resulting in it returning no data.*
9. 13th February: Frank Sinatra officially launches his own record label, Reprise Records, with the release of his single The Second Time Around. *Interesting facts: Sinatra launched Reprise in order to have more artistic freedom for his own recordings. One of the label's founding principles was that each artist would have complete creative freedom and, at some point, complete ownership of their work (including publishing rights).*
10. 15th February: Sabena Flight 548, a Boeing 707 en route from New York City, crashes near Brussels, Belgium, killing 73. The fatalities include the entire U.S. Figure Skating team who were travelling to the World Figure Skating Championships in Prague, Czechoslovakia.
11. 15th February: A total solar eclipse occurs across southern Europe.
12. 25th February: The last public trams in Sydney, Australia, cease operation bringing to an end the Southern Hemisphere's largest tramway network.
13. 26th February: Hassan II is pronounced as King of Morocco. One of Morocco's most severe rulers he remains in power until his death on the 23rd July 1999.
14. March-April: Project Mohole, an attempt in to drill through the Earth's crust, is undertaken off the coast of Guadalupe Island, Mexico.

15.	8th March: The nuclear submarine USS Patrick Henry arrives at the Scottish naval base of Holy Loch, from South Carolina in the United States, having set an underseas record by cruising submerged for 66 days and 22 hours.
16.	8th March: Aviator Max Conrad touches down in Miami setting a new world record by having circumnavigated the earth in 8 days, 18 hours and 49 minutes. Flying a PA-23 Aztec named New Frontiers, Conrad was accompanied by Richard Jennings, an observer for the record flight.
17.	9th March: Korabl-Sputnik 4, a Soviet spacecraft carrying the mannequin Ivan Ivanovich, a dog named Chernushka (Blackie), and some mice and a guinea pig, is launched from the Baikonur Cosmodrome in southern Kazakhstan. *Fun Facts: The spacecraft completes a single orbit of the earth and is successfully recovered. The mannequin Ivanovich is ejected from the spacecraft and descends separately under its own parachute.*

18. 13th March: Floyd Patterson KOs Ingemar Johansson in 6 rounds at the Exhibition Hall at Miami Beach in Florida to retain his NBA, Ring and lineal boxing heavyweight titles. *NB: This was Patterson's third consecutive fight against Johansson having previously lost his heavyweight titles to him on the 26th June 1959, and then having regained them on the 20th June 1960.*

19.	13th March: A mudslide occurs when a dam securing the loam pulp dump of a brick factory near the Babi Yar mass murder site in Kiev, Ukraine (which was then part of the Soviet Union) collapses after rain. The Soviet authorities suppress information about the disaster and claim that 145 people are killed. *Follow up: A 2012 study in Ukraine estimates the number of victims is closer to 1,500.*
20.	18th March: The 6th Eurovision Song Contest takes place at the Palais des Festivals et des Congrès in Cannes, France. The winner is Luxembourg with the song "Nous les amoureux", performed by Jean-Claude Pascal.
21.	3rd April: A Leadbeater's possum (thought to have been extinct for over 50 years) is rediscovered by naturalist Eric Wilkinson in Victoria, Australia.

22.	5th April: Eighteen-year-old Barbra Streisand makes her first television appearance in the United States on NBC's "The Jack Paar Show".
23.	11th April: The trial of Nazi Adolf Eichmann begins in Jerusalem after being captured near his home in Buenos Aires, Argentina on the 11th May 1960. *Follow up: Eichmann was convicted on 15 counts of crimes against humanity, war crimes, crimes against the Jewish people, and membership in a criminal organisation. On the 15th December 1961 he was sentenced to death by hanging and was executed a few minutes past midnight on the 1st June 1962.*

24. 12th April: Soviet cosmonaut Yuri Gagarin becomes the first human to journey into outer space after being launched from the Baikonur Cosmodrome in southern Kazakhstan aboard Vostok 1. He completes one orbit of Earth before ejecting from the descending capsule and parachuting to the ground. *Follow up: After the flight Gagarin becomes an international celebrity and is awarded many medals and titles including "Hero of the Soviet Union", his nation's highest honour. Photo: Major Yuri Gagarin waving to the crowds in London on the 11th July 1961.*

25.	17th April: Bay of Pigs Invasion: The CIA launches a full-scale invasion of Cuba by 1,400 American-trained Cubans (Brigade 2506) who had fled their homes when Castro took over in 1959. The invasion does not go well and the invasion is crushed within two days.
26.	17th April: The 33rd Academy Awards ceremony, honouring the best in film for 1960, is held at the Santa Monica Civic Auditorium in Santa Monica, California. Hosted by Bob Hope, the winners include Burt Lancaster, Elizabeth Taylor and the romantic comedy-drama film The Apartment. Jimmy Stewart accepts an honorary Oscar on behalf of his friend Gary Cooper who is too ill to attend - Cooper dies less than four weeks later on the 13th May 1961.
27.	23rd April: Judy Garland performs in a legendary comeback concert at a packed Carnegie Hall in New York City. *Interesting facts: Often referred to as the 'greatest night in show business', the concert cements Garland's legacy as one of the most powerful performers of all time.*

28.	24th April: The Swedish warship Vasa, which had sunk 1300 meters into her maiden voyage in 1628, is recovered from Stockholm Harbour. *Fun facts: The Vasa, housed at the Vasa Museum in the Royal National City Park in Stockholm, is one of Sweden's most popular tourist attractions and has been seen by over 35 million visitors since 1961.*
29.	29th April: The World Wildlife Fund (now the World Wide Fund for Nature) is established. *Interesting facts: Today the WWF is the world's largest conservation organisation and has over five million supporters worldwide.*
30.	1st May: The Pulitzer Prize is awarded to Harper Lee for her novel "To Kill a Mockingbird".
31.	5th May: Alan Shepard becomes the first American in space aboard Mercury-Redstone 3 (named Freedom 7 by Shepard). Launched from Cape Canaveral, Florida, his 15-minute suborbital flight is watched by an estimated 45 million television viewers across the United States.
32.	16th May: Park Chung-hee takes over in a military coup in South Korea. *NB: He would go on to serve as the President of South Korea from 1963 until his assassination in 1979.*
33.	18th May: At the 14th Cannes Film Festival "The Long Absence", directed by Henri Colpi, and "Viridiana", directed by Luis Bunuel, are jointly awarded the Palme d'Or.
34.	22nd May: An earthquake, covering an estimated area of 50,000 square miles, rocks New South Wales, Australia.
35.	25th May: Apollo program: U.S. President Kennedy announces, before a special joint session of Congress, his goal to put a man on the Moon before the end of the decade.
36.	26th May: A U.S. Airforce B-58 Hustler flies from New York City to Paris in a record 3h 19m 41s, covering the 4,612 miles at an average speed of 1,386mph.
37.	27th May: Using the poly-U experiment as a model, Marshall Nirenberg and Heinrich Matthaei become the first people to recognise and understand genetic code at the NIH labs on the outskirts of Washington D.C., - it is the birthdate of modern genetics.
38.	30th May: Rafael Leónidas Trujillo, a totalitarian despot who had ruled the Dominican Republic since February 1930, is killed in an ambush. His death puts an end to the second longest-running dictatorship in Latin American history.
39.	31st May: In the European Cup Final at the Wankdorf Stadium in Bern, Switzerland, Benfica beats Barcelona 3-2 to become the first Portuguese team to win the tournament.
40.	1st June: The Amhara Region of Ethiopia is hit by an earthquake with a magnitude of 6.5 on the Richter scale. Thirty people are killed and 5,000 inhabitants in are left homeless.

41. 16th June: Twenty-three-year-old Russian ballet dancer Rudolf Nureyev breaks free from Russian embassy guards at Le Bourget airport in Paris and requests asylum in France. *Follow up: Nureyev is immediately granted temporary asylum in France. Not long after settling in the West he meets up with leading British dancer Margot Fonteyn who brings him to the Royal Ballet in London (which forms his base for the rest of his dancing career). Today Nureyev is regarded by many as the greatest male dancer of the 20th century.*

42. 23rd June: The Antarctic Treaty, to ensure that Antarctica is used for peaceful purposes and international cooperation in scientific research, comes into effect.

43. 4th July: The Soviet submarine K-19 suffers a reactor leak in the North Atlantic off the south-east coast of Greenland. Under orders from the Captain the engineering crew manage to rig a secondary coolant system to avoid a reactor meltdown. *Follow up: The entire crew is irradiated and all seven members of the engineering crew, and their divisional officer, die of radiation exposure within a month. Fifteen other sailors also die over the next two years.*

44. 7th July: An explosion at the Dukla coal mine, located near the city of Havířov in Czechoslovakia, leaves 108 dead.
45. 12th July: A Ilyushin Il-18 aircraft from Zurich crashes while attempting to land at Casablanca, Morocco, killing all 72 persons on board.
46. 12th July: Two dams that supply water to the City of Pune in India burst resulting in an estimated 1,000 deaths.
47. 23rd July: Twenty-four-year-old American opera singer Grace Bumbry becomes the first black singer to perform at the Bayreuth Festival in Germany; the audience applaud for 30 minutes, necessitating 42 curtain calls.
48. 31st July: Ireland submits an application for full membership of the European Economic Community to the Council of Ministers in Brussels.
49. 6th August: Vostok 2: Soviet cosmonaut Gherman Titov becomes the second human to orbit the Earth and the first to be in outer space for more than a day.
50. 13th August: Construction of the Berlin Wall by the Communist government of the German Democratic Republic begins.
51. 21st August: Kenyan anti-colonial activist and politician Jomo Kenyatta is released by British authorities after nearly nine years of imprisonment and detention. *Follow up: Two years later, after Kenya achieves independence, Kenyatta becomes its first Prime Minister (1963-1964), and then its first President (1964-1978).*

52.	22nd August: German nurse Ida Siekmann jumps from a window in her tenement building in East Berlin trying to flee to the West. She becomes the first of at least 138 people to die at the Berlin Wall.
53.	30th August: The Convention on the Reduction of Statelessness is signed at the United Nations in New York. It does not come into effect until the 13th December 1975.
54.	10th September: During the F1 Italian Grand Prix at Monza, German Wolfgang von Trips, driving a Ferrari, crashes into a stand killing 15 spectators and himself. The race is not stopped and is won by von Trips teammate Phil Hill, who clinches the World Drivers Championship and becomes the first American F1 champion.
55.	18th September: United Nations Secretary-General Dag Hammarskjöld dies in an air crash in Northern Rhodesia whilst en route to cease-fire negotiations during the Congo Crisis. *NB: Hammarskjöld is the only person to be awarded a Nobel Peace Prize posthumously.*
56.	21st September: The Boeing CH-47 Chinook, a twin-engined, tandem rotor heavy-lift helicopter, makes its maiden flight.
57.	27th September: Sierra Leone becomes 100th member of the United Nations.
58.	3rd October: The Beach Boys record their debut single "Surfin" at the World Pacific Studio in Los Angeles. *Fun facts: The single effectively begins the Beach Boys' music career and establishes them at the vanguard of what would later be regarded as the "California Sound".*

59. 27th October: In Berlin, just two months after the construction of the Wall, a standoff between Soviet and American tanks heightens Cold War tensions. The confrontation is resolved when Soviet leader Khrushchev and U.S. President Kennedy agree to withdraw the tanks after 17 hours. In a statement concerning the Wall Kennedy declares "It's not a very nice solution, but a wall is a hell of a lot better than a war".

60.	29th October: Devrim, the first ever car designed and produced in Turkey, is demonstrated during Republic Day celebrations. *Notes: Designed and built in just 130 days, the Devrim (meaning Revolution in Turkish) was never mass-produced and became the subject of jokes for many years.*
61.	30th October: The Soviet Union detonates a 50-megaton hydrogen bomb (known as Tsar Bomba) over Novaya Zemlya in northern Russia. *Interesting fact: It remains today the most powerful human-made explosive ever detonated.*
62.	30th October: The Soviet Party Congress unanimously approves a resolution removing Stalin's body from Lenin's tomb in Red Square (as part of de-Stalinisation efforts).
63.	31st October: Hurricane Hattie devastates Belize City, the capital of British Honduras (now Belize), killing 307 and leaving more than 10,000 people homeless. *Note: In 1971, as a result of Hurricane Hattie, the capital was moved inland to the city of Belmopan.*
64.	November: Issue No.1 of Marvel Comics "The Fantastic Four" debuts (launching the Marvel Universe and revolutionising the American comic book industry).
65.	3rd November: The United Nations General Assembly unanimously elects U Thant to the position of acting Secretary-General. *NB: On the 30th November he was unanimously appointed Secretary-General, an office he would hold until the 31st December 1971.*

66. 9th November: American test pilot Major Robert Michael White sets a world record speed of 4,093mph in an X-15 experimental spaceplane, and in so doing becomes the first pilot to fly a winged craft at six times the speed of sound. *Fun fact: White officially qualified as an astronaut on the 17th July 1962 when he flew the X-15 to an altitude of 59 miles (the U.S. sets the definition of the boundary of space at 50 miles). Photo: Test pilot Bob White on the 7th February 1961 with the X-15.*

67. 17th November: Michael Rockefeller, the son of New York Governor and later U.S. Vice President Nelson Rockefeller, disappears in the jungles of New Guinea. *Follow up: Rockefeller is presumed to have died two days later after trying to swim 12 miles to shore following his pontoon boat becoming swamped and overturning. Further rumours suggest that he managed to reach the shore but was then killed and eaten by cannibals. Despite these claims no remains or other proof of his death have ever been discovered.*
68. 2nd December: In a nationally broadcast speech, Cuban leader Fidel Castro announces he is a Marxist-Leninist and that Cuba will adopt socialism.
69. 2nd December: Dutchman Anton Geesink becomes the first non-Japanese judo world champion at the World Judo Championships held in Paris.

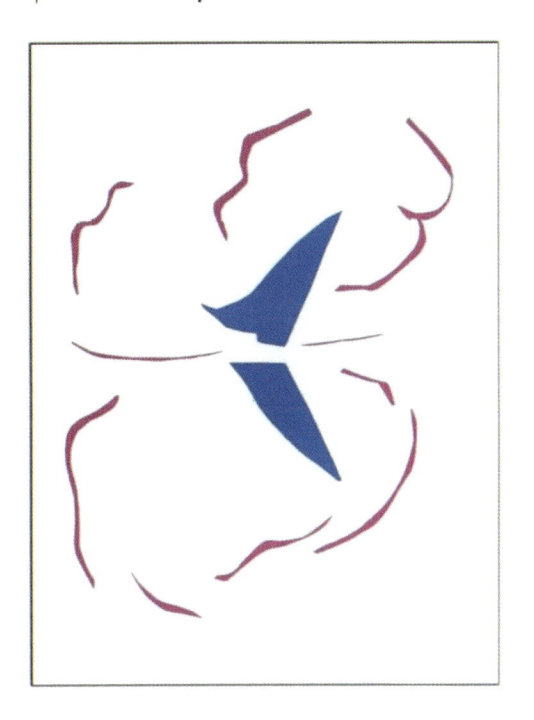

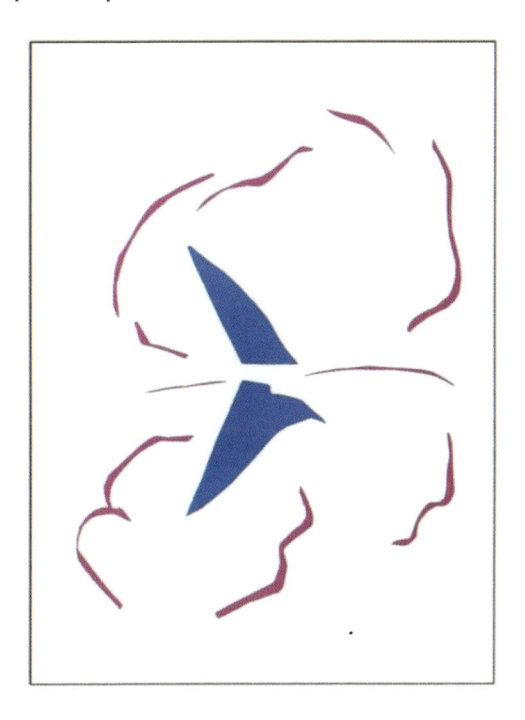

70. 4th December: French artist Henri Matisse's "Le Bateau", which had been hung upside down for 47 days by the Museum of Modern Art in New York, is finally flipped the right way up. *Pictured: A correctly orientated painting of Le Bateau by Matisse (left) vs the upside-down version preferred by the Museum of Modern Art (right).*

71. 9th December: The Australian federal election sees Robert Menzies' Liberal / Country Coalition Government re-elected with a one-seat majority (defeating the Labor Party led by Arthur Calwell).
72. 17th December: A circus tent fire in Niterói, Brazil, kills over 500 people (70% of the victims are children). *Follow up: The circus tent, imported from India, had been advertised as being made of nylon but was actually cotton treated with highly flammable paraffin wax.*
73. 19th December: The Portuguese surrender Goa, Daman and Diu to India ending 451 years of rule by Portugal over its remaining exclaves in India.
74. 19th December: The World Food Programme (WFP) is formed as a temporary United Nations program. *NB: Today the WFP is the world's largest humanitarian organisation addressing hunger and promoting food security. It provides food assistance to an average of 91.4 million people in 83 countries each year.*
75. 31st December: Ireland's first national television station, Telefís Éireann (later RTÉ), begins broadcasting.

BIRTHS

British Personalities

BORN IN 1961

Fiona Phillips
b. 1st January 1961

Journalist, broadcaster and television presenter.

Graham McPherson (Suggs)
b. 13th January 1961

Singer-songwriter, musician, radio personality and actor (Madness).

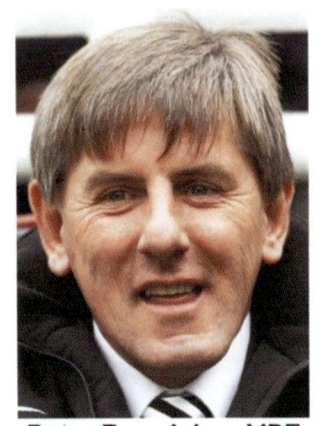

Peter Beardsley, MBE
b. 18th January 1961

Footballer who represented England 59 times between 1986 and 1996.

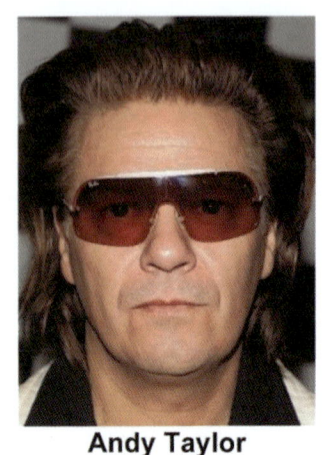

Andy Taylor
b. 16th February 1961

Guitarist, singer, songwriter and record producer (Duran Duran).

Justin Fashanu
b. 19th February 1961
d. 2nd May 1998
First openly gay professional footballer.

Fatima Whitbread, MBE
b. 3rd March 1961
World record javelin thrower and Olympic silver medallist.

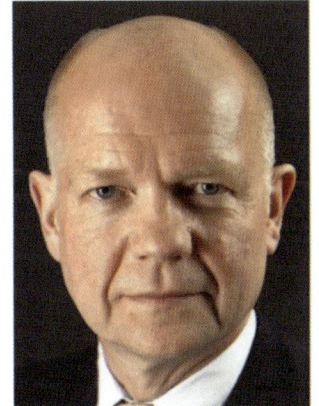

William Hague, PC, FRSL
b. 26th March 1961
Conservative politician who was the Leader of the Opposition from 1997 to 2001.

Ellery Hanley, MBE
b. 27th March 1961
Rugby league player who captained the Great Britain team from 1988 until 1992.

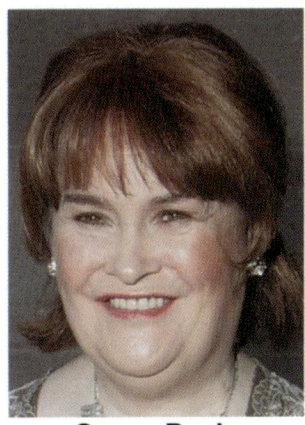

Susan Boyle
b. 1st April 1961
Singer who rose to fame after appearing on the third series of Britain's Got Talent.

Keren Woodward
b. 2nd April 1961
Pop singer, songwriter and founding member of girl group Bananarama.

Rory Bremner
b. 6th April 1961

Impressionist and comedian.

Robert Carlyle, OBE
b. 14th April 1961

Actor who starred in Trainspotting (1996) and The Full Monty (1997).

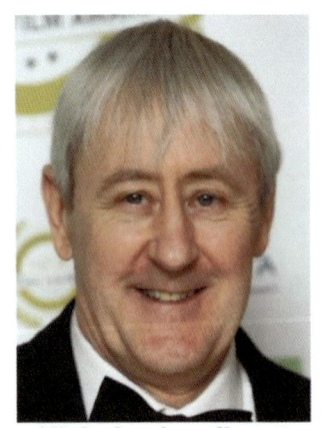

Nicholas Lyndhurst
b. 20th April 1961

Actor best known for playing Rodney Trotter in Only Fools and Horses.

Harry Enfield
b. 30th May 1961

Comedian, actor, writer and director.

George Alan O'Dowd
b. 14th June 1961

Singer, songwriter, DJ and fashion designer known professionally as Boy George.

Alison Moyet
b. 18th June 1961

Singer, songwriter and performer.

Iain Glen
b. 24th June 1961

Actor known for playing Ser Jorah Mormont in the television series Game of Thrones.

Ricky Gervais
b. 25th June 1961

Comedian, actor, writer, producer and director.

Meera Syal, CBE
b. 27th June 1961

Comedian, writer, playwright, singer, journalist, producer and actress.

Diana, Princess of Wales
b. 1st July 1961
d. 31st August 1997

First wife of Charles, Prince of Wales, and mother of Prince William and Prince Harry.

Janet McTeer, OBE
b. 5th August 1961

Tony / Olivier Award winning actress.

Brian Conley
b. 7th August 1961

Comedian, television presenter, singer and actor.

David Howell Evans
b. 8th August 1961

Musician, songwriter and lead guitarist better known as the Edge (U2).

Simon Weston, CBE
b. 8th August 1961

Army veteran known for his charity work and recovery from severe burn injuries.

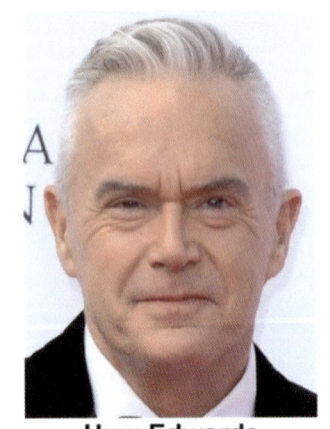

Huw Edwards
b. 18th August 1961

Journalist, presenter and newsreader.

Joe Pasquale
b. 20th August 1961

Comedian, actor and television presenter.

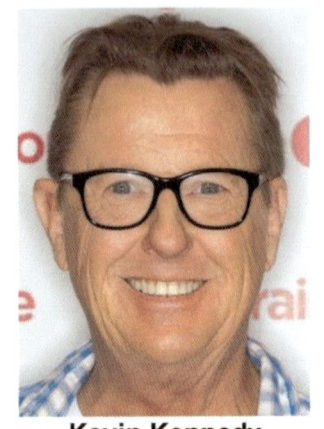

Kevin Kennedy
b. 4th September 1961

Actor and musician best known for playing Curly Watts on Coronation Street.

Caroline Flint
b. 20th September 1961

Labour Party politician who served as the MP for Don Valley (1997-2019).

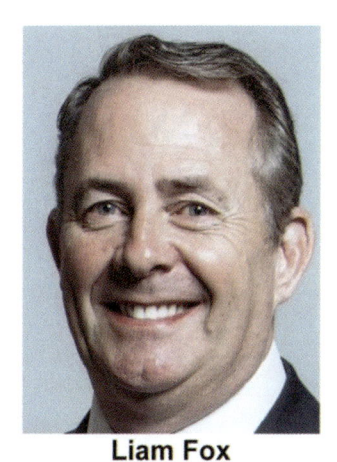

Liam Fox
b. 22nd September 1961

Conservative Party politician who has been an MP since 1992.

Jack Dee
b. 24th September 1961

Stand-up comedian, actor, presenter and writer.

Martin Kemp
b. 10th October 1961

Actor, musician (Spandau Ballet) and director.

Neil Buchanan
b. 11th October 1961

Television presenter, artist and musician.

Ian Rush, MBE
b. 20th October 1961

Footballer who represented Wales 73 times between 1980 and 1996.

Pat Sharp
b. 25th October 1961

Radio / television presenter and DJ.

Jill Dando
b. 9th November 1961
d. 26th April 1999

Journalist, television presenter and newsreader.

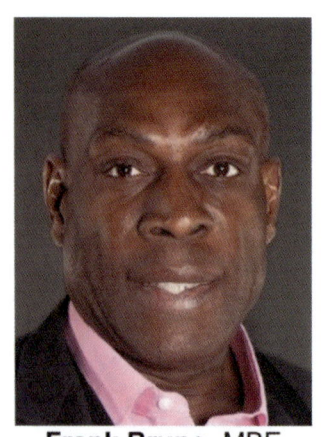

Frank Bruno, MBE
b. 16th November 1961

Professional boxer and former WBC heavyweight title holder.

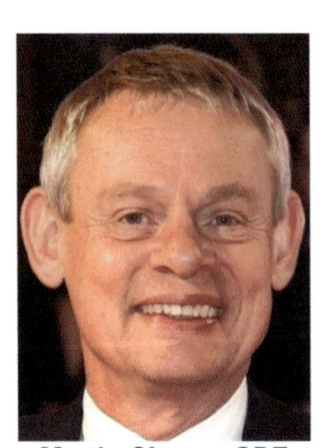

Martin Clunes, OBE
b. 28th November 1961

Actor, television presenter, film director and comedian.

Marco Pierre White
b. 11th December 1961

Chef, restaurateur and television personality.

Sara Dallin
b. 17th December 1961

Pop singer, songwriter and founding member of girl group Bananarama.

Carol Smillie
b. 23rd December 1961

Television presenter, actress and former model.

Notable British Deaths

14th Jan	Ernest Frederic Graham Thesiger, CBE (b. 15th January 1879) - Stage and film actor noted for his performance as Doctor Septimus Pretorius in James Whale's film Bride of Frankenstein (1935).
26th Jan	Morris Stanley "Stan" Nichols (b. 6th October 1900) - The leading all-rounder in English cricket for much of the 1930s.
30th Jan	John Duncan Fergusson (b. 9th March 1874) - Artist and sculptor, regarded as one of the major artists of the Scottish Colourists school of painting.
4th Feb	Air Vice-Marshal Sir Philip Woolcott Game, GCB, GCVO, GBE, KCMG, DSO (b. 30th March 1876) - Royal Air Force commander who later served as Governor of New South Wales and Commissioner of the Metropolitan Police in London.
5th Feb	Anthony Gustav de Rothschild (b. 26th June 1887) - Banker and member of the Rothschild family who in 1949 donated Ascott House, together with its art collections, to the National Trust. The donation also included the surrounding 261 acres of land plus an endowment for its upkeep.
6th Feb	Lawrence John Lumley Dundas, 2nd Marquess of Zetland, KG, GCSI, GCIE, PC, JP, DL (b. 11th June 1876) - Conservative politician who served as Secretary of State for India in the late 1930s.
7th Feb	William Duncan (b. 16th December 1879) - Actor, producer, writer and director of film serials. Duncan was Hollywood's first Scottish film star and one of the highest paid actors in the early film industry.

6th March: George Formby, OBE (b. George Hoy Booth; 26th May 1904) - Actor, singer-songwriter and comedian who became known to a worldwide audience through his films of the 1930s and 1940s. *Fun facts: On stage, screen and record he sang light, comical songs, usually playing the ukulele or banjolele, and became the UK's highest-paid entertainer. During the Second World War Formby worked extensively for the Entertainments National Service Association entertaining civilians and troops, and by 1946 it was estimated that he had performed in front of 3 million service personnel.*

8th Mar	Sir Thomas Beecham, 2nd Baronet, CH (b. 29th April 1879) - Conductor and impresario best known for his association with the London Philharmonic and the Royal Philharmonic orchestras.
12th Mar	Victor Henry Augustus "Vic" d'Arcy (b. 30th June 1887) - Olympic gold medal winning runner who competed at the 1912 and 1920 Summer Olympics.
23rd Mar	Charles Albert George "Jack" Russell (b. 7th October 1887) - One of the leading batsmen in county cricket during the period after World War I.
7th Apr	Vanessa Bell (b. 30th May 1879) - Painter and interior designer who was a member of the Bloomsbury Group.
9th Apr	George Oliver Onions (b. 13th November 1873) - Writer of short stories and over 40 novels. Onions wrote in a variety of genres but is perhaps best remembered for his ghost stories.

30th Apr	Richard H. Dale (b. 25th April 1927) - Grand Prix motorcycle road racer known as Dickie Dale.
2nd May	John Cornish White (b. 19th February 1891) - Cricketer who played for Somerset and England. White played in 15 Test matches and captained England in four of them.
4th Jun	William Thomas Astbury, FRS (b. 25th February 1898) - Physicist and molecular biologist who made pioneering X-ray diffraction studies of biological molecules.
28th Jun	Huw Owen Williams (b. 13th July 1886) - Welsh poet who wrote as Huw Menai. His poems were among the first classic works to be republished as a result of a 2004 incentive on the part of the Welsh Assembly Government.
15th Aug	William Macfarlane (b. 29th June 1889) - Scottish professional golfer who won the 1925 U.S. Open.
3rd Sep	Richard Maurice Ledingham Mason (b. 10th April 1934) - Explorer and last Englishman to be killed by an uncontacted Amazonian indigenous tribe.
16th Sep	Arthur Percy Frank Chapman (b. 3rd September 1900) - Cricketer who captained the England team between 1926 and 1931.
21st Sept	Eileen Arbuthnot Robertson (b. 10th January 1903) - Novelist, critic and broadcaster.
27th Sep	Sir William Bentley Purchase, CBE, MC (b. 31st December 1890) - Physician and barrister best known for his role in the development of Operation Mincemeat, a deception operation during the Second World War.
28th Sep	Arthur Michael Shepley-Smith (b. 29th September 1907) - Theatre, film and television actor.
13th Oct	John MacDonald MacCormick (b. 20th November 1904) - Lawyer, Scottish nationalist politician and advocate of Home Rule in Scotland.
30th Oct	Eily Malyon (b. 30th October 1879) - British stage and Hollywood film actress.
3rd Nov	Thomas Edward Flynn (b. 6th January 1880) - The Roman Catholic Bishop of Lancaster from 1939 to 1961.
25th Nov	Adelina de Lara, OBE (b. 23rd January 1872) - Classical pianist and composer.
7th Dec	Herbert John "Bert" Pitman, MBE (b. 20th November 1877) - Merchant Navy sailor who was the Third Officer of RMS Titanic when it sank on its maiden voyage in the North Atlantic Ocean on the 15th April 1912.
24th Dec	Charles Harold St. John Hamilton (b. 8th August 1876) - Writer specialising in long-running series of stories for weekly magazines. He is estimated to have written about 100 million words in his lifetime and has featured in the Guinness Book of Records as the world's most prolific author.

1961 TOP 10 SINGLES

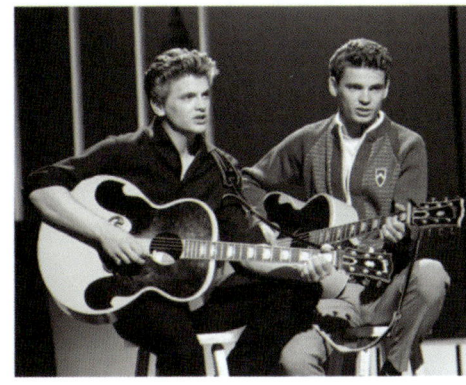

Elvis Presley	No.1	Wooden Heart
Del Shannon	No.2	Runaway
Helen Shapiro	No.3	You Don't Know
John Leyton	No.4	Johnny Remember Me
Helen Shapiro	No.5	Walking Back To Happiness
Eden Kane	No.6	Well I Ask You
The Everly Brothers	No.7	Walk Right Back / Ebony Eyes
The Allisons	No.8	Are You Sure
Billy Fury	No.9	Halfway To Paradise
Elvis Presley	No.10	Are You Lonesome Tonight?

Elvis Presley
Wooden Heart

Label: RCA Victor

Written by: Weisman / Kaempfert / Wise / Twomey

Length: 1 min 58 secs

Elvis Aaron Presley (b. 8th January 1935 - d. 16th August 1977) was a singer and actor. Regarded as one of the most significant cultural icons and influential musicians of the 20th century, he is often referred to as the King of Rock and Roll, or simply, the King. "Wooden Heart" featured in the film G.I. Blues (1960) and reached No.1 on the U.K. singles chart for six weeks in March and April 1961.

Del Shannon
Runaway

Label: London Records

Written by: Shannon / Crook

Length: 2 mins 20 secs

Charles Weedon Westover (b. 30th December 1934 - d. 8th February 1990) was a rock and roll and country musician, and singer-songwriter, better known by his stage name Del Shannon. His greatest success came with his international No.1 hit record "Runaway". Written by Shannon and keyboardist Max Crook, in 2010 it was listed at No.472 on Rolling Stone's list of the 500 Greatest Songs of All Time. Shannon was inducted into the Rock and Roll Hall of Fame in 1999.

3 Helen Shapiro
You Don't Know

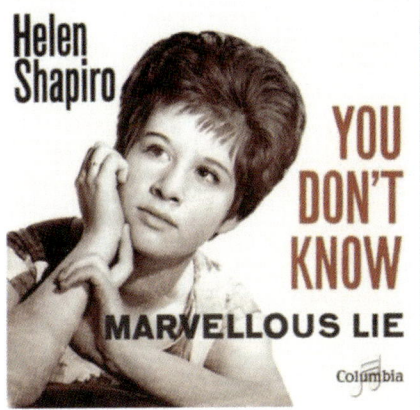

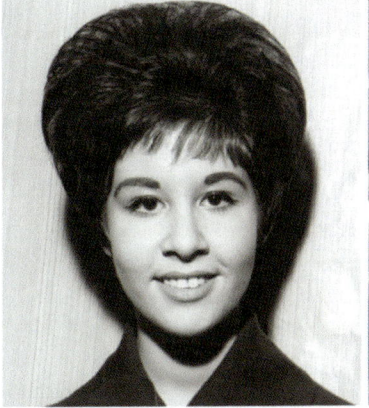

Label: Columbia | **Written by:** Schroeder / Hawker | **Length:** 2 mins 42 secs

Helen Kate Shapiro (b. 28th September 1946) is a pop singer, jazz singer, and actress whose mature voice made her an overnight sensation, as well as the youngest female chart topper in the U.K. She is best known for her two 1961 No.1 hits, "You Don't Know" and "Walkin' Back to Happiness", both recorded when she was just fourteen years old. They sold over a million copies each earning Shapiro two gold discs.

4 John Leyton
Johnny Remember Me

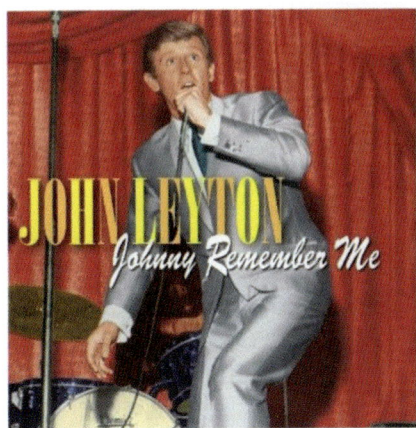

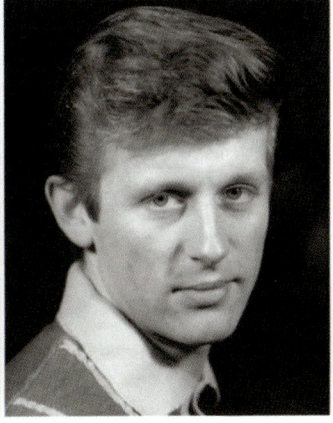

Label: Top Rank International | **Written by:** Geoff Goddard | **Length:** 2 mins 34 secs

John Dudley Leyton (b. 17th February 1936) is an actor and singer. As a singer he is best known for his hit song "Johnny Remember Me" (written by Geoff Goddard and produced by Joe Meek), which reached No.1 in the U.K. Singles Chart in August 1961 despite being banned by the BBC for its death references. His follow-up single, "Wild Wind", reached No.2 in the charts. Leyton's acting career saw him appearing in television and films throughout the 1960s (he played tunnel designer Flight Lt. Willie Dickes in 1963 film The Great Escape).

5. Helen Shapiro — Walking Back To Happiness

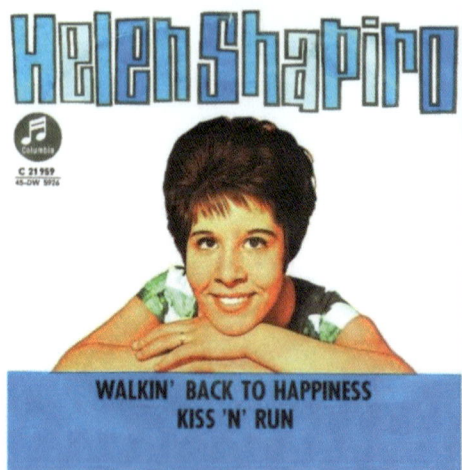

Label:	Written by:	Length:
Columbia	Schroeder / Hawker	2 mins 30 secs

Helen Shapiro was voted Britain's "Top Female Singer" before her sixteenth birthday. The Beatles' first national tour of Britain, in the late winter and early spring of 1963, was as one of her supporting acts (the Beatles were fourth on an eleven-act bill headed by the 16-year-old Londoner). By the time she was in her late 'teens, Shapiro's career as a pop singer was on the wane and she turned to cabaret appearances, touring the workingmen's clubs of North East England.

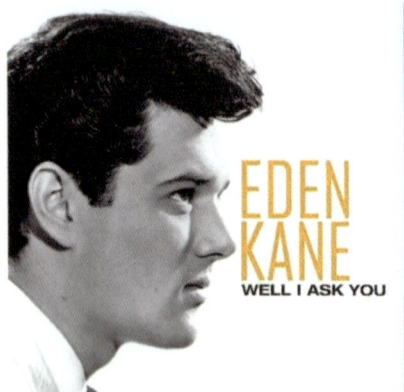

---

6. Eden Kane — Well I Ask You

Label:	Written by:	Length:
Decca	Les Vandyke	2 mins 10 secs

Richard Graham Sarstedt (b. 29th March 1940) is a pop / rock singer, record producer, actor and former teen idol known by the stage name Eden Kane. Kane had five Top 10 hits between 1961 and 1964, and together with a backing band the Downbeats, toured widely around the U.K. with such stars as Cliff Richard, Billy Fury and Helen Shapiro.

The Everly Brothers
Walk Right Back / Ebony Eyes

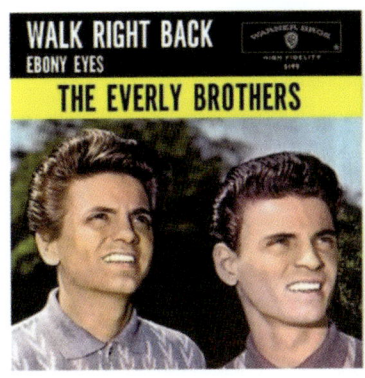

Label:
Warner Bros. Records

Written by:
Curtis / Loudermilk

Length:
2m 18s / 2m 54s

The Everly Brothers, Isaac Donald 'Don' Everly (b. 1st February 1937) and Phillip 'Phil' Everly (b. 19th January - d. 3rd January 2014), were a country-influenced rock and roll duo known for steel-string acoustic guitar playing and close harmony singing. Between 1957 and 1984 they had 30 chart singles in the UK; 29 in the Top 40, 13 in the Top 10 and 4 No.1's. The Everly Brothers were elected to the Rock and Roll Hall of Fame in 1986 and the Country Music Hall of Fame in 2001.

The Allisons
Are You Sure

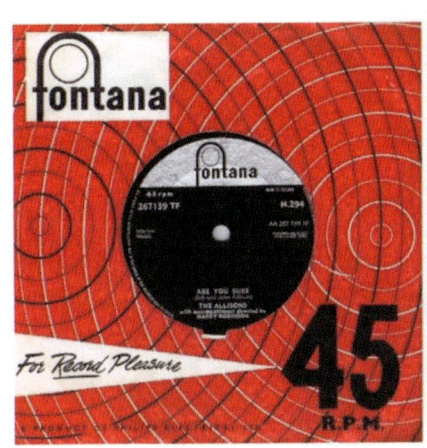

Label:
Fontana

Written by:
Bob & John Allison

Length:
2 mins 5 secs

The Allisons were a pop duo consisting of Bob Day (b. Bernard Colin Day; 2nd February 1941 - d. 25th November 2013) and John Alford (b. Brian Henry John Alford; 31st December 1939). Marketed as being brothers using the surname Allison, they represented the United Kingdom in the 1961 Eurovision Song Contest with the song "Are You Sure?" (they came second with 24 points). The song was released as a single on the Fontana label and sold over one million records, earning a gold disc. Despite a couple of minor follow-up hits the duo disbanded in 1963.

Billy Fury
Halfway To Paradise

Label: Decca | **Written by:** Goffin / King | **Length:** 2 mins

Ronald Wycherley (b. 17th April 1940 - d. 28th January 1983) was a singer, musician, songwriter and actor better known by his stage name Billy Fury. An early star of both rock and roll, and films, he equalled the Beatles' record of 24 hits in the 1960s, spending 332 weeks in the U.K. charts despite never having a No.1 single or album. Fury's version of "Halfway To Paradise" peaked at No.3, and stayed in the charts for 23 weeks to become the ninth best-selling British single of 1961.

Elvis Presley
Are You Lonesome Tonight?

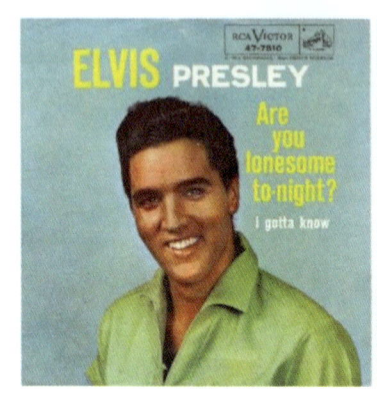

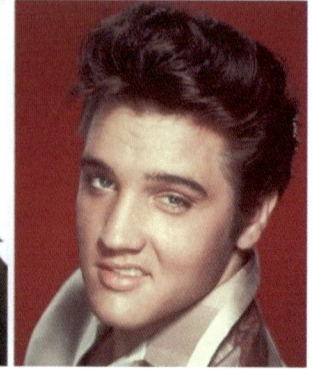

Label: RCA Victor | **Written by:** Handman / Turk | **Length:** 3 mins 7 secs

"Are You Lonesome Tonight?" was recorded (at the suggestion of manager Colonel Tom Parker) after Elvis Presley's two-year service in the U.S. Army. It was an immediate success topping the U.S. Billboard's Pop Singles chart, and a month later the U.K. Singles Chart. Commercially successful in many genres, including pop, blues and gospel, Presley is the best-selling solo artist in the history of recorded music with estimated record sales in excess 600 million units worldwide.

1961: TOP FILMS

1. **West Side Story** - *United Artists*
2. **The Guns of Navarone** - *Columbia Pictures*
3. **El Cid** - *Allied Artists*
4. **The Parent Trap** - *Disney*
5. **The Absent-Minded Professor** - *Disney*

OSCARS

Best Picture: West Side Story
Most Nominations: West Side Story / Judgment at Nuremberg (11)
Most Wins: West Side Story (10)

West Side Story Oscar winners; Chakiris, Robbins, Wise and Moreno.

Best Director: Robert Wise / Jerome Robbins - *West Side Story*

Best Actor: Maximilian Schell - *Judgment at Nuremberg*
Best Actress: Sophia Loren - *Two Women*
Best Supporting Actor: George Chakiris - *West Side Story*
Best Supporting Actress: Rita Moreno - *West Side Story*

The 34th Academy Awards, honouring the best in film for 1961, were presented on the 9th April 1962 at the Santa Monica Civic Auditorium in Santa Monica, California.

WEST SIDE STORY

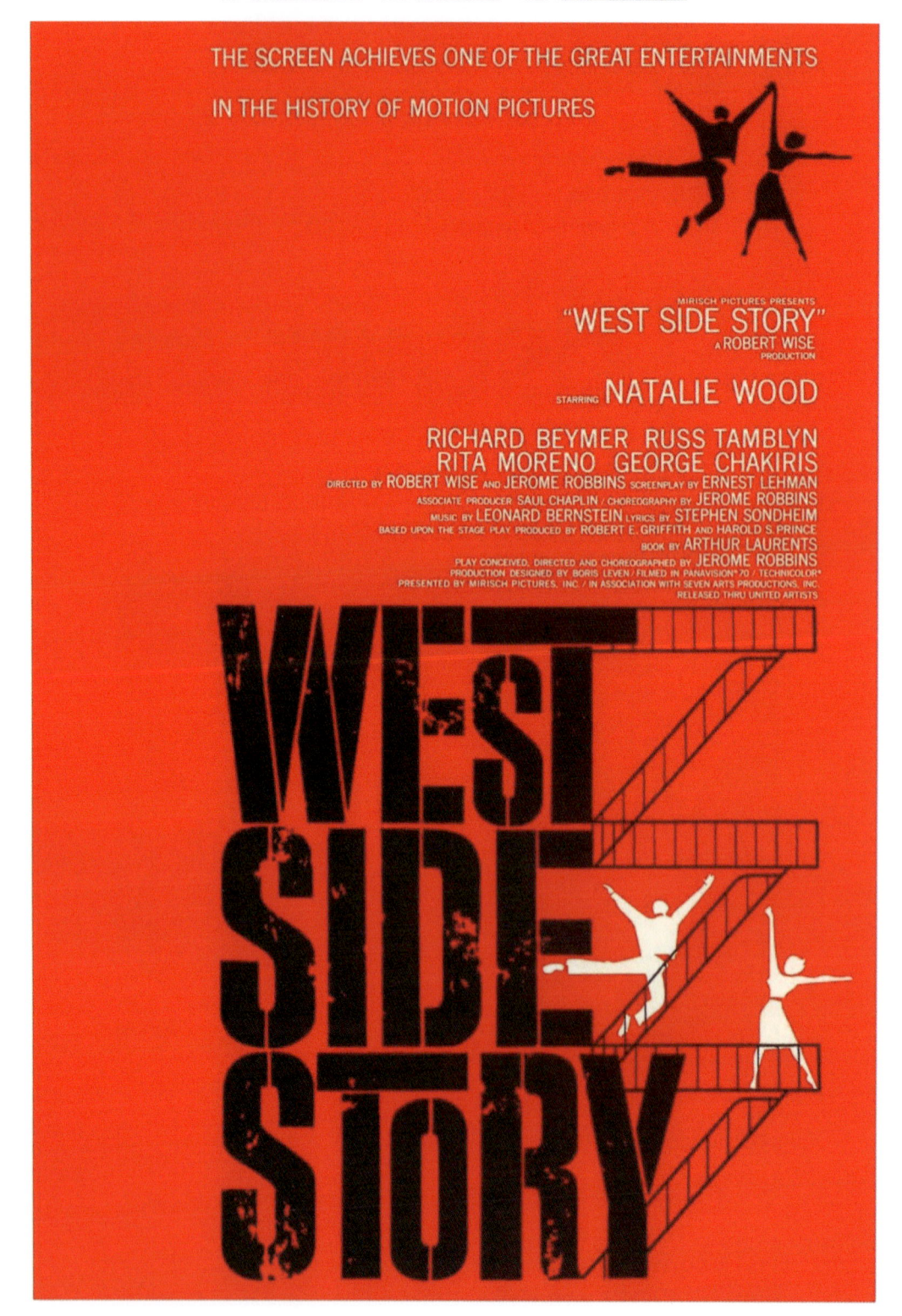

Directed by: Jerome Robbins / Robert Wise - Runtime: 2h 33min

Two youngsters from rival New York City gangs fall in love, but tensions between their respective friends build toward tragedy.

Starring

Natalie Wood
b. 20th July 1938
d. 29th November 1981
Character:
Maria

Richard Beymer
b. 20th February 1938
Character:
Tony

Russ Tamblyn
b. 30th December 1934
Character:
Riff

Trivia

Goof | Near the end of the film when Maria yells "Don't you touch him!", two different voices can be heard at the same time in the first half of the phrase (this is actually singer Marni Nixon overdubbing for Natalie Wood).

Interesting Facts | With 10 Academy Awards, West Side Story became the biggest Oscar-winning musical of all time; the previous record was held by Gigi (1958) with 9 Oscars.

Throughout the film Natalie Wood wears her trademark bracelet on her left wrist. The reason she wore bracelets was to hide an unsightly bone protrusion caused after breaking her arm in a scene in The Green Promise (1949).

Jerome Robbins initially refused to work on the film unless he could direct it. Producer Walter Mirisch was nervous about handing the reins entirely over to Robbins, who had never made a film before, so he enlisted Robert Wise to direct the drama while Robbins would handle the singing and dancing sequences. Robbins developed a habit of shooting numerous takes of each scene, to the point where the film went over budget and behind schedule. This led to him being fired, however, Robbins went on to win two Oscars, one for his Direction and one for "Brilliant Achievements in the Art of Choreography on Film".

Robert Wise's original choice to play Tony was Elvis Presley, but Presley's manager 'Colonel' Tom Parker refused as Elvis would only be singing in six of the twelve songs, and because he would not have exclusive rights to the soundtrack.

Quotes | **Maria:** All of you! You all killed him! And my brother, and Riff. Not with bullets or guns, with hate. Well now I can kill too because now I have hate!

THE GUNS OF NAVARONE

Directed by: J. Lee Thompson - Runtime: 2h 38min

A British team is sent to cross occupied Greek territory and destroy the massive German gun emplacement that commands a key sea channel.

Starring

Gregory Peck
b. 5th April 1916
d. 12th June 2003
Character:
Capt. Keith Mallory

David Niven
b. 1st March 1910
d. 29th July 1983
Character:
Cpl. John Anthony Miller

Anthony Quinn
b. 21st April 1915
d. 3rd June 2001
Character:
Col. Andrea Stavros

Trivia

Goofs | When Capt. Mallory throws the first grenade at the German patrol boat you can see the grenade still in the air as the explosion occurs.

During the ascent of the cliff face you can see the cliff face shake under the actor's weight during close-ups.

Interesting Facts | The Guns of Navarone is the only time that David Niven ever smoked cigarettes on-screen. Niven was a life-long non-smoker.

Gregory Peck often said he was disappointed that so many viewers had missed how anti-war the film was intended to be. Peck was a life-long pacifist who strongly opposed U.S. involvement in the Korean and Vietnam Wars. He was also against joining World War II until Adolf Hitler invaded the Soviet Union.

Because the stars were all too old for their characters the film was nicknamed "Elderly Gang Goes Off to War" by the British press.

The fifty-thousand-dollar fee paid to composer Dimitri Tiomkin was the highest fee paid for a single feature film score up to that time.

Quotes | **Corporal Miller:** I've inspected this vessel, and I think you ought to know that, ah, I can't swim.
Capt. Mallory: I'll keep it in mind.

[last lines]
Corporal Miller: To tell you the truth, I didn't think we could do it.
Capt. Mallory: To tell you the truth, neither did I.

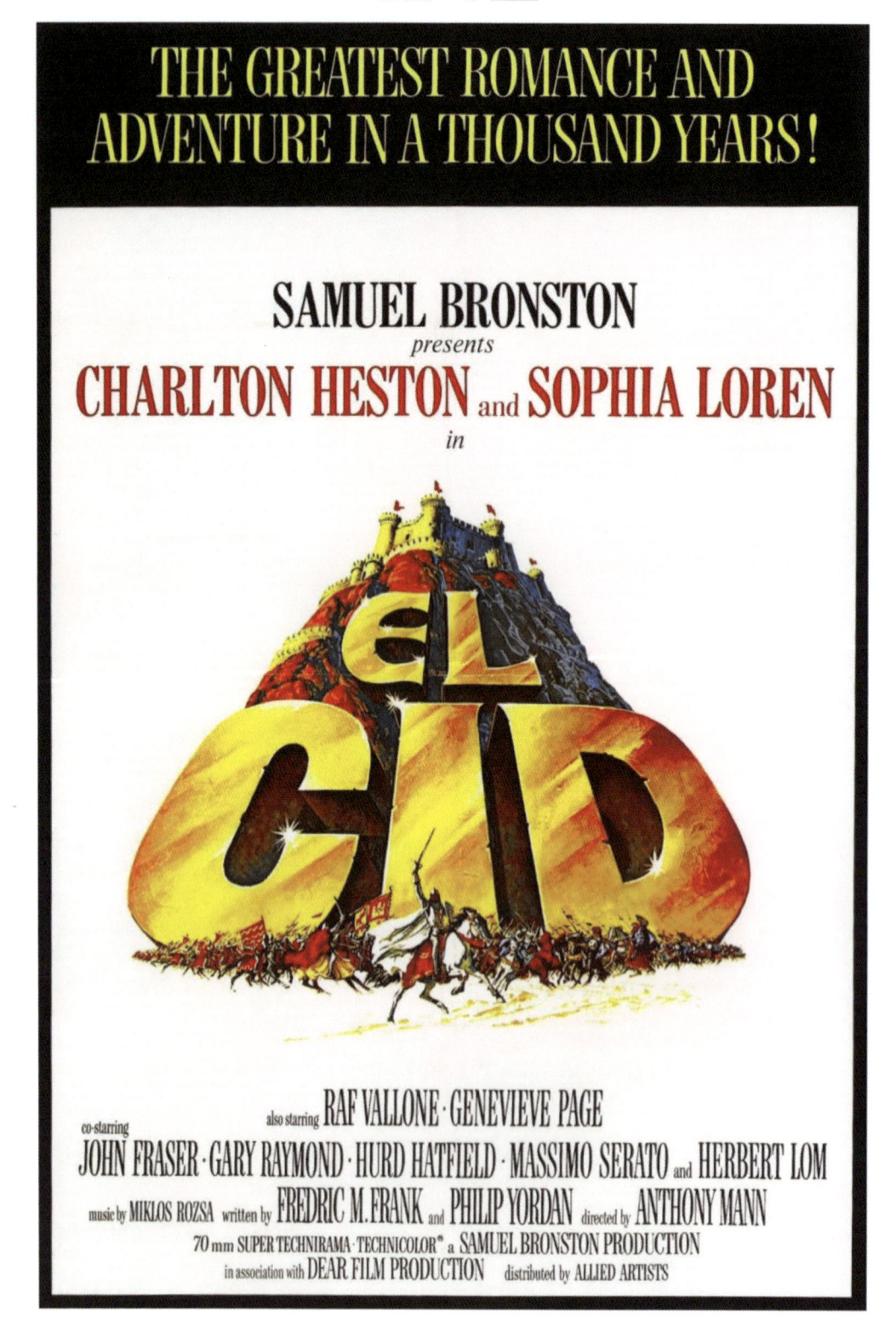

EL CID

THE GREATEST ROMANCE AND ADVENTURE IN A THOUSAND YEARS!

SAMUEL BRONSTON
presents
CHARLTON HESTON and SOPHIA LOREN
in

EL CID

also starring RAF VALLONE · GENEVIEVE PAGE
co-starring JOHN FRASER · GARY RAYMOND · HURD HATFIELD · MASSIMO SERATO *and* HERBERT LOM
music by MIKLOS ROZSA written by FREDRIC M. FRANK and PHILIP YORDAN directed by ANTHONY MANN
70 mm SUPER TECHNIRAMA · TECHNICOLOR® a SAMUEL BRONSTON PRODUCTION
in association with DEAR FILM PRODUCTION   distributed by ALLIED ARTISTS

Directed by: Anthony Mann - Runtime: 3h 2min

The fabled Spanish hero Rodrigo Diaz de Vivar (El Cid) overcomes a family vendetta and court intrigue to defend Christian Spain against the Moors.

Starring

Charlton Heston
b. 4th October 1923
d. 5th April 2008
Character:
Rodrigo Diaz de Vivar

Sophia Loren
b. 20th September 1934
Character:
Jimena

Raf Vallone
b. 17th February 1916
d. 31st October 2002
Character:
Count Ordóñez

Trivia

Goof | Alone and on horseback, Rodrigo confronts a group of mounted guards escorting the prince to a dungeon. In response to Rodrigo's demand for the release of the prisoner the captain of the guard laughingly says, "There are thirteen of us and you are alone!" In the ensuing fight Rodrigo, with some help from the prince, un-horses sixteen guards before the two remaining mounted ones flee, a total of eighteen!

Interesting Facts | Charlton Heston and Sophia Loren reportedly got off on the wrong foot early in filming which set a bad tone for their working relationship for the rest of the shoot. Heston later said he regretted the way he behaved towards Loren, feeling in retrospect that he'd been unprofessional and unfair to her, and wished he'd been kinder and less stubborn towards her.

According to Time Magazine this film required seven thousand extras, ten thousand costumes, thirty-five ships, fifty outsize engines of medieval war, and four of the noblest old castles in Spain: Ampudia, Belmonte, Peñíscola, and Torrelobatón.

A favourite of Martin Scorsese, he describes El Cid as "one of the greatest epic films ever made". Scorsese was one of the major forces behind its 1993 restoration and re-release.

Charlton Heston was the first and only choice of the producers to play El Cid (it was Heston's first starring role after winning the 1960 Academy Award for Best Actor in Ben-Hur).

Quote | **Moutamin:** In my country we have a name for a warrior with the vision to be just and the courage to show mercy. We call him... the Cid!

THE PARENT TRAP

Pop's love affair is a 3-RING CIRCUS!

WALT DISNEY presents
HAYLEY MILLS and HAYLEY MILLS

THE PARENT TRAP!
STARRING **MAUREEN O'HARA** and **BRIAN KEITH**
CO-STARRING CHARLIE RUGGLES UNA MERKEL LEO G. CARROLL JOANNA BARNES Featuring CATHLEEN NESBITT

Directed by: David Swift - Runtime: 2h 9min

Teenage twin sisters Susan Evers and Sharon McKendrick swap places in a scheme to reunite their divorced parents.

Starring

Hayley Mills	**Maureen O'Hara**	**Brian Keith**
b. 18ᵗʰ April 1946	b. 17ᵗʰ August 1920	b. 14ᵗʰ November 1921
	d. 24ᵗʰ October 2015	d. 24ᵗʰ June 1997
Character:	**Character:**	**Character:**
Susan & Sharon	Maggie McKendrick	Mitch Evers

Trivia

Goofs | Whilst singing "Let's Get Together" Sharon's hand twice momentarily disappears when it crosses over into Susan's frame.

During the close-up shot of the twins with food smeared over their faces, it is obvious one girl is not Hayley Mills, even under all the goop.

Interesting Facts | Sixteen years previously MGM had released a quickly forgotten movie called Twice Blessed (1945) whose plot was virtually identical to that of The Parent Trap.

Susan Henning took on the role as Hayley Mills' body double for many of the twin shots in the movie but as part of her contract she signed away her rights to be credited. At the wrap party Walt Disney presented her with a small statue of Donald Duck called "The Duckster" in recognition of the "best unseen performance on film".

In the shot where Mitch Evers (Brian Keith) trips on the chair, he fell so hard he cracked a rib, but like a true professional kept right on with the scene.

On its original release two Donald Duck cartoons shared the bill with The Parent Trap: Donald and the Wheel (1961) and The Litterbug (1961).

Quote | **Susan's roommate at Camp Inch:** The nerve of her! Coming here with your face!
Susan's other roommate: What are you gonna do about it?
Susan Evers: Do? What in heaven's sake can I do, silly?
Susan's other roommate: I'd bite off her nose. Then she wouldn't look like you.

THE ABSENT-MINDED PROFESSOR

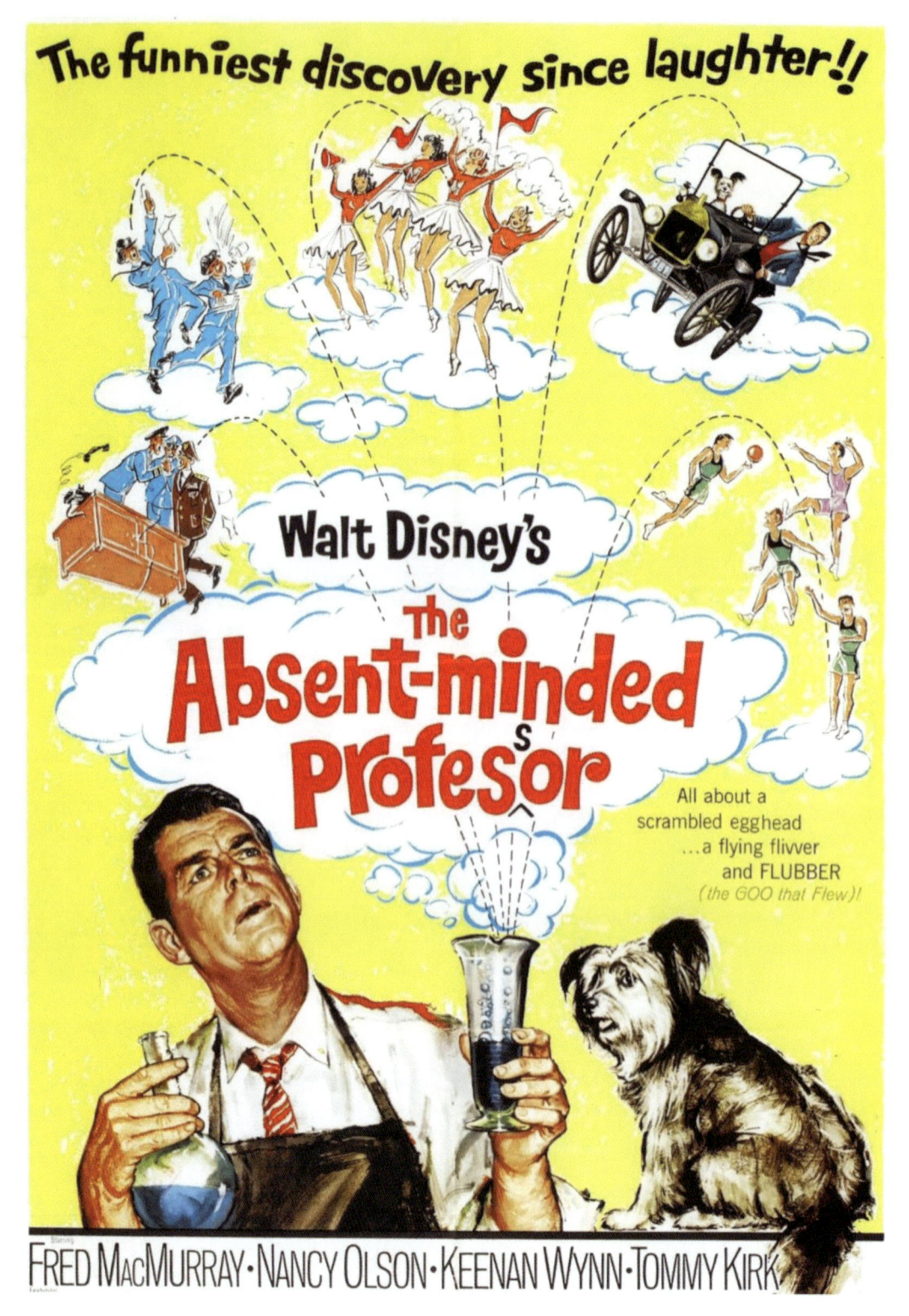

Directed by: Robert Stevenson - Runtime: 1h 32min

A college professor invents an anti-gravity substance which a corrupt businessman wants for himself.

Starring

Fred MacMurray
b. 30th August 1908
d. 5th November 1991
Character:
Professor Ned Brainard

Nancy Olson
b. 14th July 1928
Character:
Betsy Carlisle

Keenan Wynn
b. 27th July 1916
d. 14th October 1986
Character:
Alonzo P. Hawk

Trivia

Goof | When the professor is explaining to Charlie how Flubber will power the Ford Model T it is obvious that the engine and gearbox are missing from the car. When he then takes the car out for a test drive/flight the bottom view of the car clearly shows the engine and gearbox in place.

Interesting Facts | Three generations of the Wynn family act in this film: Ed Wynn, his son Keenan Wynn, and Keenan's son, Ned Wynn (uncredited part).

At the height of the film's popularity Time magazine printed the Disney special effects department's recipe for Flubber, as used in the movie. It read as follows: "To one pound of salt water taffy add one heaping tablespoon polyurethane foam, one cake crumbled yeast. Mix till smooth, allow to rise. Then pour into saucepan over one cup of cracked rice with one cup of water. Add topping of molasses. Boil till lid lifts and says 'Qurlp'." It is not recorded whether this also carried the standard warning "do not try this at home".

The legendary voice actor Mel Blanc, who voiced Bugs Bunny, Daffy Duck and Porky Pig amongst others, plays one of the firemen.

Keenan Wynn's character Alonzo Hawk returns not only in the sequel to this film, Son of Flubber (1963), but also in Herbie Rides Again (1974).

Quotes | **Professor Ned Brainard:** Mr. Hawk, let me get this straight. You want me to turn my discovery over to you so you can blackmail our government?
Alonzo P. Hawk: All right, then look at it this way, Medfield College can grow and prosper, or it can wither and die on the vine. That's entirely up to you.

Professor Ned Brainard: Let's see, flying rubber... Flubber!

SPORTING WINNERS

BBC SPORTS PERSONALITY OF THE YEAR

1961	BBC Sports Personality Results	Country	Sport
Winner	**Stirling Moss**	**England**	**Formula One**
Runner Up	Billy Walker	England	Boxing
Third Place	Angela Mortimer	England	Tennis

STIRLING MOSS - FORMULA ONE

Sir Stirling Craufurd Moss, OBE (b. 17th September 1929 - d. 12th April 2020) was a British Formula One racing driver who has been described as "the greatest driver never to win the World Championship". In a seven-year span between 1955 and 1961 Moss finished as championship runner-up four times and in third place the other three times.

Formula One Record:

Entries: 67 / Wins: 16 / Podiums: 24 / Pole Positions: 16 / Fastest Laps: 19

An inductee into the International Motorsports Hall of Fame, Moss won 212 of the 529 races he entered across several categories of competition. He competed in as many as 62 races in a single year and drove 84 different makes of car over the course of his racing career. Moss preferred to race British cars, stating, "Better to lose honourably in a British car than win in a foreign one".

Moss was made a Knight Bachelor for services to motor racing in the 2000 New Year Honours List and was knighted by Prince Charles on the 21st March 2000.

Five Nations Rugby Winners - France

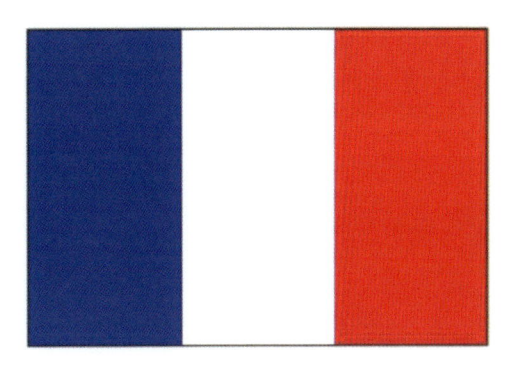

Position	Nation	Played	Won	Draw	Lost	For	Against	+/-	Points
1st	**France**	4	3	1	0	39	14	+25	7
2nd	Wales	4	2	0	2	21	14	+7	4
3rd	Scotland	4	2	0	2	19	25	-6	4
4th	England	4	1	1	2	22	22	0	3
5th	Ireland	4	1	0	3	22	48	-26	2

The 1961 Five Nations Championship was the thirty-second series of the rugby union Five Nations Championship. Including the previous incarnations as the Home Nations and Five Nations, this was the sixty-seventh series of the northern hemisphere rugby union championship. Contested by England, France, Ireland, Scotland and Wales, ten matches were played between the 7th January and the 15th April.

Date	Team	Score	Team	Location
07-01-1961	France	11-0	Scotland	Paris
21-01-1961	Wales	6-3	England	Cardiff
11-02-1961	Ireland	11-8	England	Dublin
11-02-1961	Scotland	3-0	Wales	Edinburgh
25-02-1961	England	5-5	France	London
25-02-1961	Scotland	16-8	Ireland	Edinburgh
11-03-1961	Wales	9-0	Ireland	Cardiff
18-03-1961	England	6-0	Scotland	London
25-03-1961	France	8-6	Wales	Paris
15-04-1961	Ireland	3-15	France	Dublin

Calcutta Cup

England 6-0 Scotland

The Calcutta Cup was first awarded in 1879 and is the rugby union trophy awarded to the winner of the match (currently played as part of the Six Nations Championship) between England and Scotland. The Cup was presented to the Rugby Football Union after the Calcutta Football Club in India disbanded in 1878. It is made from melted down silver rupees withdrawn from the club's funds.

Historical Records	England	Scotland	Draws
	71 Wins	40 Wins	16

BRITISH GRAND PRIX - WOLFGANG VON TRIPS

Ferrari driver "Taffy" Von Tripps receives the winner's trophy at the 1961 British GP.

The 1961 British Grand Prix was a Formula One motor race held on the 15th July at the Aintree Circuit near Liverpool. The race was won by German driver Wolfgang von Trips from fourth place on the grid over 75 laps of the 3-mile circuit. Americans Phil Hill and Richie Ginther took second and third places respectively, and the fastest lap went to British driver Tony Brooks with a time of 1m 58.7s on lap 72. This was von Trips's second and final Grand Prix victory as two races later he was killed in an accident during the 1961 Italian Grand Prix.

1961 GRAND PRIX SEASON

Date	Grand Prix	Circuit	Winning Driver	Constructor
14-05	Monaco	Monaco	Stirling Moss	Lotus-Climax
22-05	Dutch	Zandvoort	Wolfgang von Trips	Ferrari
18-06	Belgian	Spa-Francorchamps	Phil Hill	Ferrari
02-07	French	Riems	Giancarlo Baghetti	Ferrari
15-07	British	Aintree	Wolfgang von Trips	Ferrari
06-08	German	Nürburgring	Stirling Moss	Lotus-Climax
10-09	Italian	Monza	Phil Hill	Ferrari
08-10	United States	Watkins Glen	Innes Ireland	Lotus-Climax

The 1961 Formula One season was the 15th season of the FIA's Formula One motor racing. It featured the 1961 World Championship of Drivers which was contested over 8 races and was won by Phil Hill with 34 points; Wolfgang von Trips was second with 33 points and Stirling Moss third with 21 points. The season also featured the 1961 International Cup for F1 Manufacturers which was won by Ferrari.

Grand National - Nicolaus Silver

The 1961 Grand National was the 115th renewal of this world famous horse race and took place at Aintree Racecourse near Liverpool on the 25th March. Nicolaus Silver, ridden by jockey Bobby Beasley and trained by Fred Rimell, won the race by 5 lengths to become the first grey winner for 90 years.

Of the 35 horses that contested the race just 14 finished; 8 fell, 6 unseated their riders, 3 pulled up, 3 refused and 1 was brought down.

	Horse	Jockey	Age	Weight	Odds
1st	**Nicolaus Silver**	**Bobby Beasley**	9	**10st-1lb**	**28/1**
2nd	Merryman II	Derek Ancil	10	11st-12lb	8/1
3rd	O'Malley Point	Paddy Farrell	10	11st-4lb	100/6
4th	Scottish Flight II	Bill Rees	9	10st-6lb	100/6
5th	Kilmore	Fred Winter	11	11st-0lb	33/1

Epsom Derby - Psidium

The Derby Stakes is Britain's richest horse race and the most prestigious of the country's five Classics. First run in 1780 this Group 1 flat horse race is open to 3-year-old thoroughbred colts and fillies. The race takes place at Epsom Downs in Surrey over a distance of one mile, four furlongs and 10 yards (2,423 metres) and is scheduled for early June each year.

Photo: Irish-bred, British-trained Thoroughbred racehorse and sire Psidium (foaled 1958) seen being led in after winning the 1961 Epsom Derby. The horse was owned by Etti Plesch, trained by Harry Wragg and ridden by the French jockey Roger Poincelet.

Football League Champions

England

Pos.	Team	W	D	L	F	A	Pts.
1	**Tottenham Hotspur**	31	4	7	115	55	66
2	Sheffield Wednesday	23	12	7	78	47	58
3	Wolverhampton Wanderers	25	7	10	103	75	57
4	Burnley	22	7	13	102	77	51
5	Everton	22	6	14	87	69	50

Scotland

Pos.	Team	W	D	L	F	A	Pts.
1	**Rangers**	23	5	6	88	46	51
2	Kilmarnock	21	8	5	77	45	50
3	Third Lanark	20	2	12	100	80	42
4	Celtic	15	9	10	64	46	39
5	Motherwell	15	8	11	70	57	38

FA Cup Winners - Tottenham Hotspur

Tottenham Hotspur 2-0 Leicester City

The 1961 FA Cup Final took place on the 6th May at Wembley Stadium in front of 100,000 fans. Tottenham Hotspur won the match 2-0, with Bobby Smith and Terry Dyson scoring the goals. Having already won the League, Spurs became the first club to achieve the Double since Aston Villa in 1897. *Photo: Tottenham Hotspur celebrate their League and Cup Double through London in an open top double decker bus (7th May 1961).*

County Championship Cricket Winners

The 1961 County Championship, the 62nd officially organised running of this cricket competition, saw Hampshire win their first ever Championship title.

Pos.	Team	Pld.	Won	Lost	Drawn	No Decision	Bonus	Points	Avg.
1	**Hampshire**	32	19	7	6	0	32	268	8.37
2	Yorkshire	32	17	5	10	0	34	250	7.81
3	Middlesex	28	15	6	6	1	26	214	7.64
4	Worcestershire	32	16	9	7	0	24	226	7.06
5	Gloucestershire	28	11	11	5	1	18	158	5.64

The Ashes Test Series

England 1-2 Australia

Game	Date	Ground	Result
1	8th Jun - 13th Jun	Edgbaston, Birmingham	Match drawn
2	22nd Jun - 26th Jun	Lord's, London	Australia won by 5 wickets
3	6th Jul - 8th Jul	Headingley, Leeds	England won by 8 wickets
4	27th Jul - 1st Aug	Old Trafford, Manchester	Australia won by 54 runs
5	17th Aug - 22nd Aug	The Oval, London	Match drawn

Golf - Open Championship - Arnold Palmer

The 1961 Open Championship was the 90th to be played and was held between the 12th and 15th of July at Royal Birkdale Golf Club in Southport, England. Arnold Palmer won the first of two consecutive Open Championships (one stroke ahead of Dai Rees) to take the fourth of his seven major titles and £1,400 in prize money. Palmer was the first American to win the Claret Jug since Ben Hogan in 1953.

Photo: Arnold Palmer takes a few practise swings at the British Open Golf Championships at Royal Birkdale (13th July 1961).

WIMBLEDON

Photo 1: Angela Mortimer holds her trophy after defeating fellow Briton Christine Truman in the Ladies' Singles final. Photo 2: Rod Laver holds his cup up aloft after winning the Men's Singles final at Wimbledon.

Men's Singles Champion: Rod Laver - Australia
Ladies Singles Champion: Angela Mortimer - United Kingdom

The 1961 Wimbledon Championships was the 75th staging of tournament and took place on the outdoor grass courts at the All England Lawn Tennis and Croquet Club in Wimbledon, London. It ran from the 26th June until the 8th July and was the third Grand Slam tennis event of 1961.

Men's Singles Final:

Country	Player	Set 1	Set 2	Set 3
Australia	Rod Laver	6	6	6
United States	Chuck McKinley	3	1	4

Women's Singles Final:

Country	Player	Set 1	Set 2	Set 3
United Kingdom	Angela Mortimer	4	6	7
United Kingdom	Christine Truman	6	4	5

Men's Doubles Final:

Country	Players	Set 1	Set 2	Set 3	Set 4	Set 5
Australia	Roy Emerson / Neale Fraser	6	6	6	6	8
Australia	Bob Hewitt / Fred Stolle	4	8	4	8	6

Women's Doubles Final:

Country	Players	Set 1	Set 2
United States	Karen Hantze / Billie Jean Moffitt	6	6
Australia	Jan Lehane / Margaret Smith	3	4

Mixed Doubles Final:

Country	Players	Set 1	Set 2
Australia	Fred Stolle / Lesley Turner	11	6
Australia / West Germany	Robert Howe / Edda Buding	9	2

COST OF LIVING

BÉNÉDICTINE

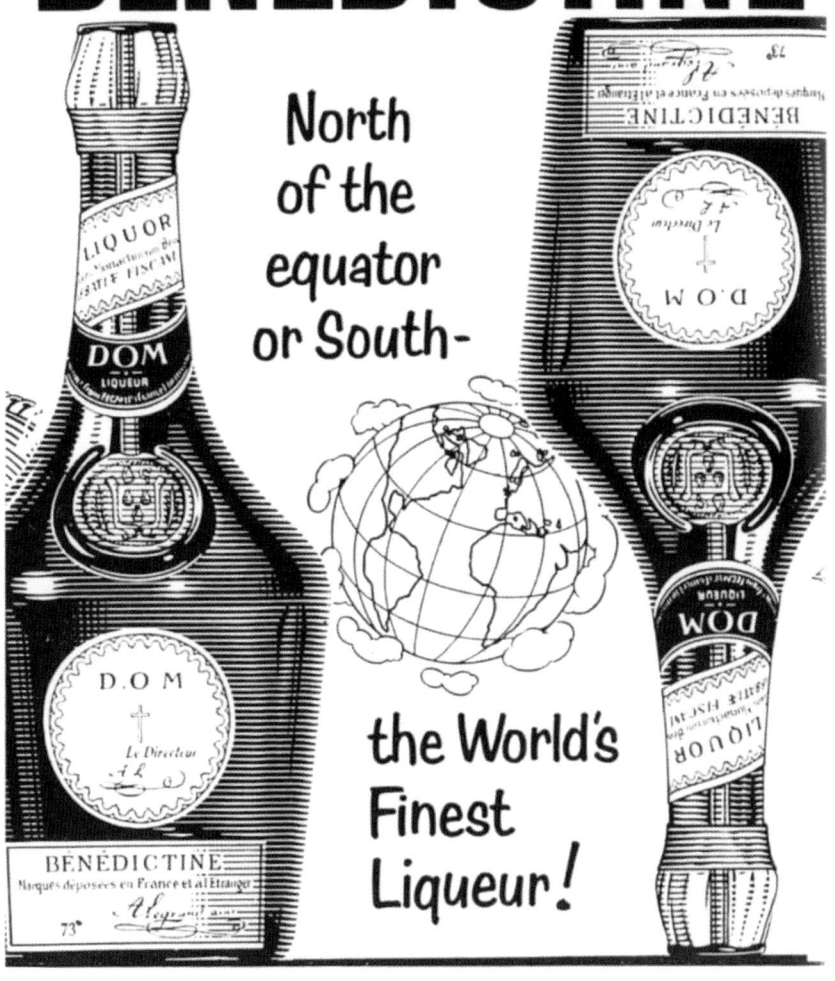

North of the equator or South— the World's Finest Liqueur!

COMPARISON CHART

	1961	1961 (+ Inflation)	2020	% Change
3 Bedroom House	£3,850	£89,500	£234,853	+162.4%
Weekly Income	£8.8s.6d	£195.85	£619	+216.1%
Pint Of Beer	1s.2d	£1.36	£3.79	+178.7%
Cheese (lb)	3s.5d	£3.97	£2.98	-24.9%
Bacon (lb)	4s.2d	£4.84	£2.94	-39.3%
The Beano	3d	29p	£2.75	+848.3%

Selected Shopping

Whipped Bon-Bons (¼lb)	5d
Liquorice Allsorts (¼lb)	4d
Hacks Medicated Sweets (¼lb)	1s
Victory V Lozenges (pkt.)	6d
Romance Milk Chocolate Bar	9d
Cadbury's Roses Chocolates (½lb box)	5s.6d
Norfolk Turkey	from £1.15s
Chickens	from 6s
Colman's Mustard Powder	6d
CO-OP Christmas Pudding	1s.3d
Spree Orange / Lemon Squash (sachet)	4d
CO-OP Ninety Nine Tea (¼lb)	1s.9d
Nescafe Instant Coffee (8oz tin)	11s.9d
Peek Frean's Shortcake Biscuit (pkt.)	11½d
Coronette Hair Styling Spray	3s.6d
Coronette Hair Lacquer	3s.6d
Old Spice Aftershave	6s.2d
Eucryl Tooth Powder	1s.11½d
Eucryl Pure Bristle Toothbrush	3s.9d
Cutex Hand Cream	3s.7d
Cleer Nose Spray	3s.9d
Beecham's Constipation Pills	2s

BIRDS EYE VEGETABLES
– THEY'RE READY PREPARED!

BIRDS EYE
BRUSSELS SPROUTS
GARDEN PEAS
SLICED GREEN BEANS
CRINKLE CUT CHIPS

Eat Better with Birds Eye

WEEK-END SHOPPING IDEA

New Zealand Lamb*

Serve a tender joint of New Zealand lamb this weekend. A leg or shoulder makes a splendid roast. It's plentiful now and so reasonably priced!

*It's nicer with Mustard!

PIC-NIC READY MIXED 8½d. 1/2d.
POWDER READY-TO-MIX 6d. 11d. 1/7d.

CLOTHES

Women's Clothing

West-End Mink-Dyed Marmot Coat	49gns
Corot Furs Real Nylon Coat	16gns
Smartwear Pakamac	6s.4d
J.A. Davis & Son Chic Dress 'n' Jacket	£3.3s
Ashley Knitwear Pure Wool Cardigan	£1.4s
Scott & Reed Tricel Pleated Dress	£1.12s
Woollen Mixture Pinafore Dress	19s.11d
Floral Printed Cotton Housefrock (x2)	18s.11d
Bridget Pencil Skirt	£2.2s.6d
Weargood Ladies Cavalry Twill Slacks	£1.15s
Lace Trimmed Sleeveless Nighties (x2)	15s.11d
Ambrose Wilson Freeform Corselette	£2.2s.6d
New Moon Sling Bra	£1
Cellular Briefs (x6)	9s.11d
Morley Seamfree Nylon Stockings	from 4s.11d

Chic from every angle

MELANIE 24/11
Tropic

KANGOL

London and Cleator / look inside \ for the label

Men's Clothing

Indiana Gaberdine-Weave Raincoat	£1.9s.11d
U.S.A. Forces G.I. Baseball Cap	3s.8d
British Naval Pure Wool Jersey	19s.6d
Double Two Cotton Poplin Shirt	£1.19s.6d
Ex-Admiralty White Collar Shirt (x6)	5s.11d
Nylon Re-Inforced Trousers	19s.11d
Fairway House Dressing Gown	£1.8s.6d
Wildsmith & Co. Ready To Wear Shoes	£11.11s
Montfort Airlift Nylon Mesh Socks	3s.11d

TOYS

Phillips 3-Speed Sports Bicycle	£18.6s
Wendy Playhouse	£3.9s.11d
Airfix Construction Kits	from 2s
Dinky A.A. Patrol Van	4s.11d
Corgi Aston Martin D.B.4 Saloon	4s.7d
Hornby Dublo Freight Locomotive & Tender	£4.7s.7d
Lego Fire Station Special Box	19s.9d
Junior Pears Encyclopaedia	13s

"This is 1961, chaps—must have gears on our bicycles!"

GEARS LIKE A CAR
—fitted neatly in the back hub—it's
MARVELLOUS!

This is the "jet" age—a chap **must** have gears on his bicycle. Who has ever heard of a "one-gear" car? Sturmey-Archer give you a "gearbox" in its most wonderful form—tucked in the back hub, fully enclosed and as utterly reliable as any mechanically minded chap would want. On your new bicycle—see that you've got Sturmey-Archer.

STURMEY-ARCHER GEARS, LTD., NOTTINGHAM.

STURMEY ARCHER

ELECTRICAL ITEMS

Murphy 19in B&W Television / VHF Radio	92gns
Lacknu Ltd. Tuneable Transistor Radio	11½gns
Rolls Electric Central Heating	79gns
Electric Convector Heater	19s.11d
Easiclene Two-Five Fridge	46gns
Rolls Super 66 Twin Tub Washer Dryer	39gns
Pifco Electric Blanket	£4.6s.4d
Tarpen Electric Chainsaw	£28
Sunbeam Shavemaster	£11.18s.8d
Horstman Dog Clippers	15gns

OTHER PRICES

Rover 100 Car	£1,538
Vauxhall Victor Car	£862
Austin Super Seven Car	£592
Triumph Sports Cub 200cc Motorcycle	£164
Thorn Built Concrete Garage	from £38.7s
Champion Spark Plugs (each)	5s
15 Day Italian Sunshine Holiday	£28.9s
10 Day Sunny Spain Coach Tour	18gns
8 Days Cosmos Tour Paris	13gns
8 Days Full Board Belgium	£8.15s
1 Week Pontins Seaside Holiday	from £8.10s
Portable Washing Wringer	£2.5s
Kitchen Table + 2x Chairs & 2x Stools	£7.10s
Shackleton Single Divan Bed	8½gns
Witney Blanket Double Spring Mattress	£7.7s
Albemarle Carry-Cot	£1.9s.11d
Cosiglow Hot Water Bottle	5s
7'6" x 5' Luxurious Woven Carpet	£4.19s.6d
Denhill Skymaster 10x50 Binoculars	£13.19s.6d
21 Jewel Razor Edge Automatic Watch	£6.15s
Swiss 17 Jewel Waterproof Watch	£4.7s.6d
Dewar's White Label Whisky	£2.1s.6d
De Kuyper Cherry Brandy	£1.16s
Seager's Cream Australian Sherry	10s
Hungarian Balatoni Riesling Wine	9s.6d
Guards Cigarettes (20)	3s.6d
Churchman Olympic Cigarettes (20)	2s.10d
Woodbines (50)	8s.6½d
Colibri Monogas Cigarette Lighter	£3.8s.6d
Woman's Realm Magazine	5d

Wonderful whisky for Christmas

"White Label"

Scotch Whisky by **DEWAR'S** *- it never varies*

Play like the maestro with a Frido ball

Stanley Matthews, the world's most famous footballer, recommends Frido vinyl balls. He uses them himself! They're tough, hardwearing, re-inflatable, and the types shown here are repairable too. Frido balls are perfect for training—they're more lively than a leather ball and super for improving your ball control.

THE FRIDOMASTER	THE 'A' BALL	THE GYM BALL	THE RUGBY BALL
F.A. regulation size and weight — 16 oz. — in brown or white. Repairable and re-inflatable.	Size 8½". Weight 8½ ozs. In red or white. Repairable and re-inflatable.	Size 8½". Weight 10 ozs. In orange. Repairable and re-inflatable.	Regulation size. Weight 12 ozs. In brown or white. Repairable and re-inflatable.

FROM SPORTS OUTFITTERS AND TOY SHOPS EVERYWHERE

NOW OUTSELLS ALL COMPETITORS COMBINED

3'6 TWENTY

In three years, Guards have become outstandingly successful cigarettes. Now they account for more than half the filter cigarettes selling at similar prices.

People are changing to Guards for two good reasons: Guards' unbeatable quality and the rich, true flavour of finest Virginia tobacco. *Guards are a man's choice.*

Pimms makes a bowled batsman blissful
Pimms makes a duck seem well played
Pimms is the star at the after-match bar
Add lemonade and it's made.

PIMMS

The No. 1 PARTY DRINK

Pimms plus fizzy lemonade, topped with a slice of lemon, looks fun, tastes delicious

Send for Pimms Party leaflet to: Pimms, 100 Bishopsgate E.C.2

1961 Money Conversion Table

Pounds / Shillings / Pence 'Old Money'		Decimal Value	Value 2020 (Rounded)
Farthing	¼d	0.1p	2p
Half Penny	½d	0.21p	5p
Penny	1d	0.42p	10p
Threepence	3d	1.25p	29p
Sixpence	6d	2.5p	58p
Shilling	1s	5p	£1.16
Florin	2s	10p	£2.32
Half Crown	2s.6d	12.5p	£2.91
Crown	5s	25p	£5.81
Ten Shillings	10s	50p	£11.62
Pound	20s	£1	£23.25
Guinea	21s	£1.05	£24.41
Five Pounds	£5	£5	£116.23
Ten Pounds	£10	£10	£232.47

How luxurious can an Austin Seven get?

Most people are very nicely satisfied thank you with *any* Austin Seven. Others want the earth. The new Austin Super Seven has been designed for them. It's got everything any other Austin Seven's got—high m.p.h. (70), high m.p.g. (50), large space inside (for seating four adults), small-space outside (for parking in 11 feet). *And it's got much more. Here's what.*

INSIDE New duotone trim in subtly blending colour-choices. Sound insulation to hush the engine to a gentle purr. Fuller cushions for greater comfort: thick new carpets. New oval-shaped instrument panel, including both oil-pressure and water-temperature gauges. And many many more extras.

OUT New duotone palette of brilliant colours to choose from. Much more dashing fine-mesh grille. It's altogether a gayer, brighter car. Add up the list of improvements when you see the new model at your Austin dealer. Price: £405 plus £186.17.3 Purchase Tax and surcharge

GET INTO AN AUSTIN AND OUT OF THE ORDINARY

NEW AUSTIN SUPER SEVEN

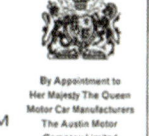

THE AUSTIN MOTOR COMPANY LIMITED · LONGBRIDGE · BIRMINGHAM

By Appointment to Her Majesty The Queen Motor Car Manufacturers The Austin Motor Company Limited

Backed by BMC 12-month warranty and BMC service

CARTOONS

Laughter

"Supa-Dupa Cookers? What do you dial to boil a kettle?"

"Mum! I got that new washing machine I promised you."

'I must ask you, Miss Ardent, to confine your campaigning to out-of-shop hours'

Printed in Great Britain
by Amazon